THE BOOK ON ESTIMATING REHAB COSTS

THE BOOK ON
ESTIMATING REHAB COSTS

The Investor's Guide to Defining Your Renovation Plan, Building Your Budget, and Knowing Exactly How Much it All Costs

REVISED EDITION

J SCOTT

BiggerPockets® PUBLISHING

The Book on Estimating Rehab Costs, Second Edition
J Scott

Published by BiggerPockets Publishing LLC, Denver, CO
Copyright © 2019 by ScottBuilt, LLC.
All Rights Reserved.

Publisher's Cataloging-in-Publication data

Names: Scott, J., author.
Title: The book on estimating rehab costs : the investor's guide to defining your renovation plan, building your budget, and knowing exactly how much it all costs, revised edition. / J Scott.
Description: Denver, CO: BiggerPockets Publishing, LLC, 2019.
Identifiers: LCCN 2018957550 | ISBN 9781947200128 (pbk.) | 9781947200135 (ebook)
Subjects: LCSH Housing rehabilitation--Economic aspects--United States. | Real estate investment. | BISAC BUSINESS & ECONOMICS / Real Estate / General | BUSINESS & ECONOMICS / Real Estate / Buying & Selling Houses.
Classification: LCC HD255 .S37 2019 | DDC 333.33/83--dc23

Second Edition

Published in the United States of America
10 9 8 7 6 5 4 3

To my awesome boys, Chase and Cade, who give me a reason to get out of bed each morning—and then give me a reason to crawl back into bed each night, completely exhausted.

I love you guys.

J Scott

TABLE OF CONTENTS

Welcome to the Second Edition 8

SECTION 1
Introduction 11
How to Use this Book 12
Factors that Impact Rehab Costs 14
Methods of Estimation 16

SECTION 2
The Framework 19
The 25 Renovation Components 19
Format of Discussion 20
A Word About Cost Estimates 22

SECTION 3
The Components 25
Component #1: Roof 26
Component #2: Gutters, Soffit, and Fascia 34
Component #3: Siding 40
Component #4: Exterior Painting 48
Component #5: Decks and Porches 53
Component #6: Concrete 58
Component #7: Garage 62
Component #8: Landscaping 66
Component #9: Septic System 72
Component #10: Foundation 75
Component #11: Demo 79
Component #12: Plumbing 83

Component #13: Electrical 100
Component #14: HVAC 112
Component #15: Framing 123
Component #16: Insulation. 127
Component #17: Sheetrock 132
Component #18: Carpentry—Doors, Windows, Trim 139
Component #19: Interior Painting 144
Component #20: Cabinets and Countertops 148
Component #21: Flooring 154
Component #22: Permits 164
Component #23: Mold. 169
Component #24: Termites. 176
Component #25: Miscellaneous 181

SECTION 4
Putting it All Together 185

Acknowledgements. 196

About the Author 199

WELCOME TO THE SECOND EDITION

It's been nearly six years since the original edition of this book was published, and for anyone who has been active in the real estate industry during that time, it shouldn't surprise you that there have been some drastic changes.

When I wrote the first edition back in 2012, we were in the very early stages of recovering from the Great Recession and the 2008 housing crash. Prices of both renovations and real estate itself had bottomed out, and we were starting an upswing in most markets. But there was no way I could have predicted that just a few short years later, we'd be riding a housing wave that is surpassing what we saw back in 2005 and 2006.

In many aspects of the economy, the recovery has been slow and methodical; but in real estate, the upswing has been sharp and dramatic. According to the Bureau of Labor Statistics, the number of construction workers in the U.S. increased nearly 50 percent between 2011 and 2016—and this doesn't account for unlicensed contractors and the small, independent workers many investors are accustomed to working with.

Given these changes in the industry, I felt it was time for an update to this book. If you're familiar with the first edition, you're likely to notice the following industry-wide changes reflected in the second edition:

- **Labor prices have increased considerably, especially in the areas of carpentry and other skilled trades.** The biggest shift in the real estate industry since the Great Recession has been in the labor market. After the 2008 downturn, the vast majority of contractors had gone out of business or left the industry, and the handful of remaining professional contractors were struggling for work. This led to artificially low prices for renovation work. In the past ten years, the labor market has rebounded, and prices have increased to higher than pre-recession levels. In many areas, labor prices have increased 50 percent or more since 2013, especially with skilled and artisan contractors.

- **Material prices have increased for non-commodity items.** While not as drastic as labor price increases, materials prices in some areas and for some specific types of materials have increased dramatically over the past decade. Due to inflation, increased demand, and external factors such as international trade negotiations, the cost of most non-commodity materials has increased, and the cost of some materials including steel, lumber, and paint has increased considerably. Luckily, the cost of many commodities including fasteners and fixtures has increased very little, if at all.

- **Price ranges around the country are now more consistent, with smaller ranges.** After the 2008 recession, there was a good bit of discrepancy between renovation pricing in areas that stood up well to the housing crash and areas that got hit hard by the crash. It wasn't uncommon for renovation tasks to be several times more expensive in one area compared with another. But with the current revitalization in housing, prices across the country have started to converge a bit more. For reasons we'll discuss later in the book, you'll still find that contractor prices in some places—California and New York City, for example—are several times higher than most of the rest of the country, but for about 90 percent of the markets in the U.S., prices are now more consistent than they used to be.

- **Smaller jobs and lower-cost tasks have increased in price more quickly than larger jobs and higher-end tasks.** Contractors are no longer desperate for work, and in many cases, contractors have so much work that they can pick and choose what jobs they want to take. It should come as no surprise that, given a choice, contractors will choose larger and more expensive jobs over smaller and less expensive ones. It takes about the same amount of marketing and sales time to acquire a small job as a large one, so focusing on the larger jobs makes basic economic sense. For homeowners and investors, this means that finding contractors for smaller and lower-cost jobs is both more difficult and more expensive than it used to be.

My goal with this second edition is twofold:

1. **Update the prices and price ranges for each of the renovation components in the book.** To do this, I surveyed dozens of active and successful investors from around the country, not only to get an accurate assessment of their labor and material prices, but also to get an idea of what types of contractors they're using and how they are completing their renovations.

2. **Provide additional tips to help with the inspection of the various renovation components.** One of surprise takeaways from the feedback I received on the first edition was that many readers found the book to be a great introduction not only to creating a scope of work and a renovation budget—the intended goals of the book—but also a primer on how to do inspections with the goal of understanding which components needed to be repaired and which were in working condition. In the second edition, I have attempted to provide even more detail around how to inspect many of the components we discuss, hopefully making your job as an investor even easier.

I hope you find the updates to this book valuable, and I wish you good luck on your first—or next—renovation!

SECTION 1
INTRODUCTION

For ten years, I've been writing about my adventures of rehabbing houses on my blog, 123Flip.com. In that time, I've received thousands of comments, messages, emails, and phone calls from new and experienced investors—not just rehabbers but landlords, wholesalers, and commercial investors as well.

While I get lots of questions regarding every aspect of investing, a common theme of those messages and discussions has been the difficulty real estate investors have with figuring out what rehab tasks to undertake and then estimating the costs of completing those renovations.

And I can relate! When I first started rehabbing houses, I had absolutely no real estate or construction experience. I could barely change a light bulb. I remember walking into my first potential rehab projects, looking around and thinking to myself, "Where do I start? What am I looking for? What questions should I be asking? How much is this going to cost me?"

After spending several years putting together and putting into practice my methodology for analyzing rehab projects, I've decided to document the process I use so that I can help other investors who I know are in the same situation I was in several years ago.

How to Use this Book

If you're like me, you probably want to skim over this introductory section and jump right into the meat of the text. That's what I'd probably do. But I'm going to ask that you take a few minutes to read this section in full, as it may make the difference between your being enlightened by the rest of the book or frustrated by it.

I want to start with a few tips on how to use this book. In fact, these are more than just tips; these are also important disclaimers about what this book can and can't do for you. Here they are:

- Many of you are likely reading this book to learn how to accurately estimate the cost of renovations for your rehab projects. In fact, many of you noticed the title of the book and have already thought to yourself, "I'll skim the part about creating a scope of work (SOW) and jump right to the good stuff—the estimation process!" That would be a mistake. As you'll quickly learn in this business, your SOW and your budget are inescapably intertwined, and without learning the gory details of creating a SOW, you'll never get proficient at learning to estimate rehab costs.

- This book will provide a framework for thinking about the tasks associated with renovation projects and the range of costs associated with each of those tasks. While I provide over 100 of the most common renovation tasks, some of you may be in a situation where you think to yourself, "You didn't touch on half the things I need to do in my rehabs!" You may be correct. In certain parts of the country and with certain types of houses, there are going to be renovation tasks applying to a small handful of investors that don't apply to the broader demographic. Unfortunately, even if I knew all the nuances of rehabbing in every location and every type of house, I couldn't fit all that information into one book. Instead, my goal here is to give you a *framework* for thinking about your renovation tasks so that you can ask the appropriate questions of your contractors and other investors with whom you network.

  Additionally, while I will provide cost ranges for the most common renovation tasks, these ranges may not be accurate for all rehabbers, for all properties, for all locations and for all situations. In fact, you may look at the cost lists and think to yourself, "Everything in my area is more expensive than that!" Or you may think to yourself, "I can do all those things for half the cost you indicate!" And you may be absolutely correct. What I've found is that while material prices aren't too drastically different around the country if you shop around for suppliers, and labor prices are surprisingly consistent (within 25 percent to 35 percent) throughout much of the United States, there are many exceptions.

For example, material prices will be much higher in parts of the country where there are impediments to delivery and high tariffs or taxes. And while labor prices tend to be relatively consistent (again, within a range of about 25 percent to 35 percent) for much of the country, there are some areas where prices could be twice the high end of my ranges. For example, in parts of California, New York, New Jersey, and other high-cost-of-living locations, you may find that labor prices are outside the boundaries I lay out in this book. This is also true for areas that are heavily union controlled, though union members will tend to do side work at pretty good prices. As such, learn my methodology, but in some cases, take my numbers with a grain of salt.

- Your goal while reading this book is to get an understanding of the methodology I use to create a SOW and estimate rehab costs. After reading this book, your homework will be to determine what other tasks are common in your area and with your type of rehabs, and also to determine the actual labor and material prices for each of these tasks based on all the factors specific to you and your business. In each section, I will give you pointers on how to find local prices, as well as how you should be paying for the work when the time comes to actually hire contractors.

Remember, no matter what anyone might tell you or try to sell you, there is no magic formula for being able to determine what you should renovate on a particular house or how much the renovation will cost. Learning how to put together a realistic SOW and create an accurate budget takes preparation, practice, and experience. There are no shortcuts. As I mention above, I probably can't give you all the answers you seek, but I can tell you what questions you need to ask, to whom you need to direct these questions, and what to do with the information you receive.

If you use this book as intended, and if you put in the time and effort to learn the entire process of generating a SOW, research your local prices, and then generate your rehab estimates based on a detailed SOW, you'll find that you have a huge advantage over the majority of rehabbers out there. In my experience, very few rehabbers—including many of the "professionals"—have a detailed methodology for planning their renovation projects and estimating their renovation costs. For that reason, these unprepared rehabbers consistently find themselves over budget on projects and making smaller profits than they had projected... and sometimes they don't make any profit at all!

With those disclaimers out of the way, let's jump into it!

Factors that Impact Rehab Costs

I mentioned earlier that I can't give you all the answers within these pages, especially when it comes to the cost of your rehabs. The reason for this is simple: The cost of your renovations is going to differ greatly from the cost of my renovations and the cost of everyone else's renovations. Even if you, I, and ten other investors were to purchase the exact same house, our costs would likely be very different.

Here are just a few things that will impact the cost of a particular renovation:

- **Location:** Renovations cost different amounts in different locations. Both material and labor prices are going to vary based on where you do your projects. I do projects in multiple cities, and in each city, my prices are different. Granite in Atlanta, Georgia, costs me $28 per square foot; the same granite in Milwaukee, Wisconsin, costs me $38 per square foot. The cost of an electrician in Los Angeles, California, is likely to be up to 30 percent higher than an equally skilled electrician in Austin, Texas. Where you do your projects will have the largest impact on the price you pay for your labor and materials.
- **Contractors:** Different contractors will charge different prices. This may have to do with their level of skill, their level of self-worth, how busy they are, or any number of other reasons. The fact is, unless you're using the same contractors I am, your prices will be different than mine. In fact, even if you use the exact same contractors I use, your prices are likely to be different than mine. If your painter is an artisan, you're likely to pay more than if he were an unskilled worker advertising on Craigslist. Do your contractors carry licenses and insurances? If so, they're likely to be much more expensive than if they don't. Not to mention the fact that your negotiating skills could mean a significant difference in what you pay the exact same contractor.

- **Level of Finish:** Are you putting in $1.50 per square foot vinyl flooring in your kitchens or $6.00 per square foot solid oak hardwoods? Are you using $40 showerheads from Home Depot, or $300 multi-jet shower massagers? Will you be letting your buyers provide their own appliances, or will you be outfitting your custom kitchen with $15,000 in upgraded stainless steel appliances? The level at which you finish your property can make a *huge* difference in the cost of your renovation, both in terms of labor and materials.

- **Specifics of the House:** As you can probably imagine, a 100-year-old Victorian in an historic neighborhood is not going to cost the same to renovate as a 15-year-old stick-built cookie-cutter in a typical suburban neighborhood. Not only are the levels of finishes different, but you're likely to run into local preservation requirements, the need for artisan contractors who know how to maintain the original style of the house, or various upgrades in electrical and plumbing based on new building codes. The various types of houses and the specific houses you work on will have a large impact on the costs you pay for your renovation. Even the fact that you may be working on an historic property will encourage contractors and vendors to hike up their prices, as they probably assume you're wealthy and have no problem spending big bucks on your renovations.

- **Time of Year:** If you want to get great labor prices, hire some carpenters in upstate New York in the dead of winter. With nobody starting renovation projects in two feet of snow, these guys are desperate for work and would rather get paid minimum wage than not get paid anything at all. Of course, try to hire an HVAC contractor at the same time and place, and you're likely to be paying an arm and a leg. With residential furnaces working overtime, and people at risk of dying if their furnace breaks, HVAC contractors can make a great living during the cold winter months. Depending on what contractors you need to hire and what time of the year you need them, your labor prices are likely to have some wild swings.

- **Building Codes:** Building codes will vary by area, often due to differences in climate, severe weather risks, soil types, geologic threats, and a host of other circumstances that require buildings to be constructed in a way that is both safe and comfortable for occupants. If you live in an area with conditions such as exceptionally hot or cold temperatures, an increased risk for tornados or earthquakes, or has suboptimal soil conditions, you'll likely find that the building codes in your area are more stringent than in many other areas of the country. These stringent building codes will often translate to higher building and repair costs, meaning you'll spend more on your rehabs than your counterparts in other areas.

While these are some of the big ones, there are many other factors that will affect the prices you pay for your renovations. With that in mind, you can see why it would be impossible for me to tell you how much you should be paying for any particular renovation task. What I can do is provide you a methodology for determining how much *you* will pay for *your* renovation projects given all the items above that are going to be specific to you alone.

Keep reading, and you'll see what I mean!

Methods of Estimation

There are many ways to estimate renovation costs. Some are easier than others, while some are more accurate than others. In fact, there is a direct correlation between simplicity and accuracy when it comes to estimating rehab costs. Here are a few of the common estimation techniques I've seen rehabbers use for their projects:

Estimating by Square Footage

Many rehabbers will estimate their renovation costs based on the size of the property. They'll come up with a per-square-foot renovation price, multiple that by the size of the house, and use the result as their estimate. This method can actually work pretty well *if* (and that's a big "if") the rehabber has a lot of experience doing that specific level of renovation on that specific type of house.

For example, I know that if I do a basic interior cosmetic renovation (such as painting, replacing carpet, changing out light fixtures and plumbing fixtures, installing new cabinetry and appliances) on one of my typical houses (3-bedroom, 2-bathroom, 2-story traditional style, built after 1990) in the suburbs of Atlanta, Georgia, with my crew of contractors, it will cost about $16 per square foot. In other words, if I were to do this type of renovation on a 1,500-square-foot house in my area, I would expect to pay about $24,000.

That number would be surprisingly accurate for me, as I've done so many similar projects that I know what my average costs are per square foot. Unfortunately, if I changed any of the variables (level of rehab, type of house, location, set of contractors), everything would change, and I'd have no idea what the per-square-foot price of the renovation would be. And if you were to call me and give me all the details of your project, asking what I would recommend in terms of per-square-foot pricing (I get this type of call all the time), I wouldn't be able to help you, as I wouldn't have nearly enough information.

Because of that, for new investors this type of estimation technique is unreliable, and I don't recommend for them.

Estimating by Room Costs

The next most common estimation technique I hear new investors discussing is per-room renovation costs. For example, an investor might ask me, "I'm renovating a house and it needs the kitchen and the master bathroom totally gutted. How much should the kitchen and one bathroom cost me?"

If you've read everything I've written in the first few pages of this book, you know by now that there's absolutely no way I can offer any insight into the cost of redoing a room without much more information. Personally, I've rehabbed houses where I've completely redone the kitchen for $5,000 and I've done other houses where the same type of renovation cost over $25,000! The houses were different, the location was different, the finishes were different, and the contractors were different.

Again, for new investors—and even for experienced investors—I wouldn't recommend this estimation technique. There are too many variables to be able to accurately assign a cost to renovating a specific room in an unknown house.

Breakdown Estimation

The third renovation estimation technique I see used is what I call *breakdown estimation*. This is the method I use and what most experienced rehabbers I know use. It involves walking the property and determining line item by line item, in gory detail, what needs to be renovated, and then assigning a cost to each line item on your list.

This methodology takes the longest to learn and requires the most work, but it provides the most accurate estimates, by far. And the nice thing about this technique is that it can be streamlined without losing accuracy. Once you master this estimating technique, you'll be able to walk through a potential house and in ten minutes be able to come up with a cost estimate that should be within 5 percent of what you will actually pay for the renovation.

I use this methodology for my rehab estimations and this is the methodology I will present in detail throughout the rest of this book.

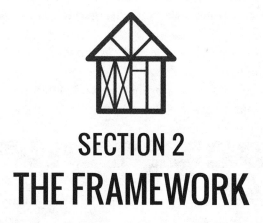

SECTION 2
THE FRAMEWORK

Every successful rehabber will have his or her own framework for evaluating the scope of a potential deal and estimating renovation costs. In this chapter, I'll present the framework I use; in the following chapters, I'll go into detail on each part of the framework and how you can use this framework to evaluate the scope and estimate the rehab costs for your potential deals.

The 25 Renovation Components

Our framework involves breaking up the property into each of its primary functional components and then evaluating each of those components individually and in detail. The framework breaks up the exterior of the property into ten major components, breaks up the interior of the property into 11 major components, and then evaluates four other general components that are a combination of interior and exterior pieces.

Within each of these major components are many tasks and subtasks that address the various renovation items that might need to be performed on each component as part of a comprehensive property renovation. Each of these tasks and sub-tasks will make up the scope of work for the renovation, and the cost estimate of each task and sub-task will contribute to the overall cost estimation for the property. This is framework I will use throughout the rest of this book.

While I can't include every renovation task you'll ever encounter here (there are too many of those for a book even ten times this size), I will include the most common tasks you will run into on typical single-family renovations.

If you're confused, keep reading. I promise it will all become clear. Now let's get started!

First, here are the 25 major property components we will consider as part of our evaluation and cost estimation:

EXTERIOR COMPONENTS	INTERIOR COMPONENTS	GENERAL COMPONENTS
1. ROOF	11. DEMO	22. PERMITS
2. GUTTERS/SOFFIT/FASCIA	12. PLUMBING	23. MOLD
3. SIDING	13. ELECTRICAL	24. TERMITES
4. EXTERIOR PAINTING	14. HVAC	25. MISCELLANEOUS
5. DECKS/PORCHES	15. FRAMING	
6. CONCRETE	16. INSULATION	
7. GARAGE	17. SHEETROCK	
8. LANDSCAPING	18. CARPENTRY	
9. SEPTIC SYSTEM	19. INTERIOR PAINTING	
10. FOUNDATION	20. CABINETS/COUNTERTOPS	
	21. FLOORING	

Format of Discussion

When evaluating scope and estimating costs, I suggest that you consider each of these components one by one; once you have completed the evaluation for each of the 25 components, you should find yourself with a detailed SOW for the project, which can then be used to generate your renovation budget estimate.

The rest of this book will be used to detail each of these 25 major components, including basic inspection techniques, how to determine SOW tasks, and how to determine the cost of implementing each of those SOW tasks.

Here is the format I'll use to detail each of the 25 components:

Overview

This section will overview the component, including how it works, what you should be looking for to determine what renovations might be required, and providing some general tips and tricks for how to optimize your renovation of this component, if necessary.

Inspection Tips

This section will provide some tips and tricks to help you determine the condition of the component and whether renovation work might be recommended or required.

Life Expectancy

This section will overview the life expectancy of the component, including any nuances that will factor into the life expectancy.

Scope of Work (SOW) Tasks

In this section, I'll detail the potential SOW tasks you should consider for the particular component being discussed. You can cut and paste the tasks that are required for your property into your master SOW to complete your scope of work.

While I will attempt to be comprehensive in the list of potential tasks, keep in mind that there may be some SOW tasks that are unique to your area, your type of property, or your situation. I will cover all the most common and most typical SOW tasks for each component, but I would highly recommend that if you have any doubts as to whether other work is required, you bring in a professional to evaluate further.

TASK 1	Detailed overview of Task 1 to help you determine if this task should be added to your SOW.
TASK 2	Detailed overview of Task 2 to help you determine if this task should be added to your SOW.

Cost Guidelines

In this section, I'll detail the factors that contribute to the cost of the component, and I will discuss the cost of implementing each of the individual tasks, broken down by labor and materials, when appropriate. As I mentioned earlier in this text, the cost of each task will vary based on a number of factors, but I'll provide a rough range of prices that should be accurate for most properties in most locations around the country.

In the final section of this book, I'll provide a cost spreadsheet listing each of the tasks for each of the major components. I would encourage you to work with local contractors to determine what your local prices will be. Once you have firm prices from your local contractors for each of these tasks, building a detailed renovation budget for any SOW you create should be simple and straightforward.

TASK 1	**$MIN - $MAX expected cost for Task 1** Other factors that might affect the price of this task or that you should be familiar with when getting contractor bids.
TASK 2	**$MIN - $MAX expected cost for Task 2** Other factors that might affect the price of this task or that you should be familiar with when getting contractor bids.

Determining Your Local Prices

In this section, I'll recommend what contractors you'll want to speak with in your local area in order to get specific pricing for your jobs, and how to approach those contractors.

How to Pay for the Job

Lastly, in this section, I'll discuss how you should expect to pay for work on this component, including what is standard in terms of upfront payments and payment schedules.

A Word About Cost Estimates

For each and every task, I'll provide a pricing estimate in the form of a price range. While I have done my best to ensure that this price range is accurate for the bulk of the locations, property types, and typical renovations done around the United States, the price ranges I provide will never be accurate in every location and for every situation.

Here's a bit more detail about how I determined these price ranges and how you should be using them.

The price ranges I provide are for typical low- to mid-level rehabs in locations where rehab prices are neither depressed nor inflated. If you skimp on quality, choose to hire contractors who aren't licensed or insured, or live in an area where real estate labor is overly depressed, it's quite likely you can find labor and materials cheaper than the minimum that I indicate. Likewise, if you're doing a higher-end rehab or live in an area where real estate costs are sky high, it's very possible that you'll find prices are above the range that I indicate. My only suggestion is that if you're finding prices that tend to be higher than the range I indicate, then do some extra research to ensure that the prices you're getting are typical for investor-level labor and materials. Just because you're getting lots of bids higher than the price range I indicate doesn't mean you should be paying those higher prices; it's quite possible you just haven't yet found investor-friendly contractors who will provide the pricing you should be getting.

For some tasks, I provide a single price range that combines labor and materials. For other tasks, I break out the labor and the materials costs into two separate price ranges. In the cases where you should expect the contractor to provide all materials for the job as part of the bid, I provide a combined labor and materials estimate. In the cases where you should seriously consider providing the materials yourself, I have broken out the labor and materials ranges separately. In some cases, I'll suggest that the contractor provide all materials, but you'll decide (either by yourself or in conjunction with your contractor) that you'd prefer to provide the materials yourself; in other cases, I'll suggest that you provide the materials, but you and your contractor will determine that an all-in bid makes more sense. Both of these situations are fine—in either case, the total cost of the bid will fall within the range of the labor and materials combined.

Also keep in mind the price ranges I provide assume no extra work or surprises related to something specific about your rehab. For example, in the very first rehab I did, I chose to put engineered hardwood throughout the living and dining rooms. I estimated $4 per square foot for the labor and materials for the hardwood installation, which was accurate, but I failed to recognize that the subfloor in that house was made of a material that wouldn't allow me to easily place hardwoods on top of it. Ultimately, after factoring in the replacement of the subfloor, my total costs came to nearly $6 per square foot, 50 percent more than I had estimated and budgeted!

These are the types of surprises and specific circumstances that can't be predicted by reading a book, which is why I always recommend being conservative in all your numbers to account for these types of surprises. Once you have a few rehabs under your belt, you'll find you're good at predicting these situations, and the surprises are fewer and further between, and also a lot less costly.

In summary, let me say this:

This book should only be used as a guideline for estimating the cost of your rehabs and should not be relied upon as your sole estimating resource. Until you are comfortable doing your estimates yourself, I highly recommend that you bring in a qualified general contractor or individual sub-contractors to provide you with detailed bids before committing to the project.

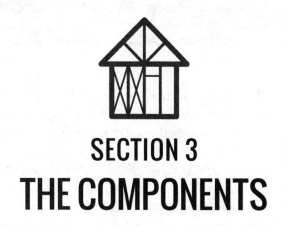

SECTION 3
THE COMPONENTS

COMPONENT #1
ROOF

Overview

There are several kinds of roofs in use today, and the types of roofs you'll see on your houses will vary based on where you live, the climate, the age of the homes, and a number of other circumstances. The most common types of roofs these days are:

- **Asphalt**. This is the typical three-tab or architectural shingle that is most common across the United States. The shingle itself may be felt, paper, or some composite material, which is then covered with asphalt and small granules, which reflect UV light from, and prevent breakdown of, the asphalt covering.
- **Wood shingles/shakes.** Wood shingles, which are typically made of cedar, were the roofing material of choice in older homes, but due to its cost is less common today than asphalt shingles.
- **Metal.** These types of roofs are becoming more popular, but they're rarely used in residential construction. While the cost is more than asphalt and other types of common roofing material, metal roofs can last a long time. Some metal roofing comes in patterns that are more appropriate for residential buildings, but unless most other homes in the area have metal roofs (or there is another reason why metal must be used), I wouldn't recommend using it.
- **Clay.** In certain parts of the country, clay roofing is very popular. Depending on your area and the architecture of your house, clay may be the preferred roofing material, but this is typically only true in the southwest United States. Clay roofs are expensive, and because they are very heavy, require proper structural support prior to installation.
- **Slate.** These roofs are very high quality and can last a long time—up to 100 years or more. But materials and installation costs are very high, and as such, this type of roofing material is not very common these days. Unless you have an historic home, you probably won't be dealing with slate roofs.

The roof of a house serves three primary purposes:
1. Keep water from coming in through the ceiling.

2. Keep water from running down the exterior walls and getting them wet.

3. Provide pleasing aesthetics to the exterior of the property.

As a rehabber, you should be concerned about the roof if it fails to serve any of these three purposes. The most common point of failure for roofs is any place where the roof changes direction (peaks and valleys) and where objects penetrate the roof (vent pipes, chimney, satellite dishes, etc.) Oftentimes, when it appears that a roof is leaking, the leak is actually not coming through the shingles, but is instead coming from a weak point in the roof:

- **Gutters:** The most common reason for a roof to appear to be leaking is clogged gutters. Water will fill the gutters, and with no other place to go, it will start to move under the roof edges of the house. When you see stains on the ceiling of the interior of the house near the exterior walls, these are often the result of gutter issues, and not roof issues (or perhaps a combination of both).

- **Flashing:** The next most common reason for a leaking roof is poor flashing—the material installed around any roof exposures to keep water from getting through the roof. If the roof is otherwise in good shape, you can often remediate roof leaks by ensuring that the flashing at all exposures is in good shape and water isn't penetrating or getting underneath the flashing.

If you have roof leaks that aren't the result of gutter issues or flashing issues, it's likely that at least part of the roof has reached its end of life, and that probably means the whole roof will need to be replaced.

Inspection Tips

Replacing or repairing a damaged roof is one of the costlier renovation tasks, and any unexpected or surprise roofing costs associated with a rehab can significantly impact your budget. In addition, a damaged or old roof can quickly lead to expensive interior renovations as well.

For this reason, I recommend spending a good bit of time looking at the roof from the best vantage point you can find and being conservative when it comes to potential issues. Don't hesitate to bring in a qualified roofer if you have any reason to believe there might be a roof issue or if you don't have the ability to decide on your own.

1

While water intrusion into the house is an obvious sign of roof damage, there are other things you should be looking for when determining the condition of a roof and whether repair or replacement is needed:

- Asphalt roofs will have several key indications when they reach the end of their service life: bare spots on the shingles, major discoloration or bleaching of the roof, large number of granules in the gutters, missing shingles, or curling at the edges of the shingles.

- Wood roofs will be more prone to splitting or rotting than asphalt roofs. If you are investigating a wood roof, look for rot (especially on lower parts of the roof where water may sit); curled, missing or split shingles; or moss growing on the roof, which is an indication of water not properly draining off.

- Due to sun exposure, south and west faces of roofs are generally most prone to wearing out, so these should be the parts of the roof that are examined most closely. On wood roofs, take notice of the north face of the roof, as less sun means longer exposure to moisture, which will wear the wood more quickly.

- Any roof surfaces beneath tree branches are prone to damage, and debris on the roof can trap water, causing the roofing materials to degrade prematurely. If you have trees overhanging the house, be sure to check those areas of the roof most closely for impact damage.

- For houses with asphalt shingles, some homeowners (and unfortunately, some rehabbers) will try to save money on demo and haul-away of the original roof by installing a second—or even a third—layer of roofing material over the original. Not only do multiple layers of roofing generally invalidate a warranty, but most roofs aren't designed to support the weight of multiple layers of shingle, and multiple layers can cause damage to the structural components of the roof. If you can get on or near the roof, check the edges and corners to see if there are obvious signs of multiple layers of shingles, and if so, have the roof inspected by a licensed roofer.

- Finally, you'll notice that many roofs have vents or other mechanisms for allowing fresh air into the attic space, reducing heat and moisture buildup that can age a roof prematurely. Any roof that doesn't allow air circulation beneath it will tend to age faster, and the evidence of damage to the shingles will appear much sooner. If the roof doesn't have proper ventilation, you probably want to scrutinize the condition a little bit more thoroughly.

As you get more experienced with your inspections, you'll find that assessing roofs gets much easier. Soon enough, you'll find that you're able to get a pretty good idea of roof condition as you pull into the driveway, before you even get out of the car.

Life Expectancy
Different roofing materials generally have differing life expectancies:
- Asphalt shingles: 20-30 years.
- Wood shingles/shakes: 40-50 years if properly installed; however, if installed over cheaper plywood sheathing (as is more common these days), roofs can deteriorate in as little as 10-20 years.
- Metal roofs: 50-100 years.
- Slate roofs: 100+ years.
- Clay roofs: 50+ years.

Because asphalt shingle is the most popular type of shingle, a good general rule of thumb to follow is this: If your house is between 15 and 30 years old and has an asphalt roof, it's probably never had the roof replaced, and probably needs it. In fact, any time I plan to look at a house built between 1980 and 1995, I assume it will need a new roof even before I look at the house. I'm right about 90 percent of the time.

Scope of Work (SOW) Tasks
While roofing systems can be pretty complicated, from a rehabber's point of view they are actually pretty simple. For 95 percent of the roofs you encounter, your renovation tasks will include one of the following:

ROOF MAINTENANCE	For roofs that have not reached end of life, a qualified roofer will walk the entire span of the roof, fixing minor items as he goes. This includes fixing flashing issues, repairing nail pops (nails that are protruding from the shingle that may allow water to penetrate), and nailing down loose shingles. Even a few missing or damaged shingles shouldn't be too much of an issue, assuming the roof isn't overly discolored and matching shingles can be found to replace the missing or damaged ones.

REPLACE SHEATHING	Generally, between the roof framing/structure and the roof covering there's a layer of wood sheathing—OSB or plywood. If water permeates the roof covering, it can damage the wood sheathing and the sheathing will need to be replaced when the roof is replaced. You can generally get a good idea of the condition of the sheathing and how much might need to be replaced by looking up at the underside of the roof from inside the attic. The sheathing is what you're looking at, and if its water stained or otherwise damaged, it will likely need to be replaced.
ROOF REPLACEMENT	For roofs that are end of life or have damage beyond a few shingles, replacement is probably necessary. A qualified roofer will remove the existing roof, replace the various roof layers (sheathing, underlayment, shingle), replace the pipe boots (the vent pipes that extrude from the roof), and reflash all openings. A typical roof replacement shouldn't take more than one or two days for a qualified crew.

Cost Guidelines

The size of a roof is generally measured in unit called a "square." A square is 10' × 10', or 100 square feet. As an example, a flat roof that measures 28 feet long by 25 feet wide would be 700 square feet in area, which roofers call 7 squares.

Unfortunately, it's often difficult to determine an exact amount of area that a roof encompasses because there are multiple different surfaces and most roof surfaces are pitched to some degree. That said, I'll typically multiply the length of the house by the width of the house and then multiple the result by two to get an approximation of the square footage of a typical roof. Mathematically, this number should be a little bit higher than the actual roof size but being conservative is always a good thing.

As an investor, it can sometimes be cheaper to purchase roofing material yourself and then pay for labor, a dumpster, and haul-away; but in my opinion, the savings aren't worth the additional time and overhead of having to coordinate materials and haul-away. I prefer to let a qualified roofing contractor handle the entire operation from beginning to end.

Next, I provide the cost you should expect to pay a qualified roofer, including both labor and materials into one price. If you would prefer to buy the materials yourself, I would recommend pricing out per-square roofing materials and then requesting a labor-only quote from local roofers—most will be happy to provide this. Keep in mind that if you decide to get a labor-only quote, you should determine if the quote includes a dumpster for haul-away of debris or whether that is an additional cost you will incur.

ROOF MAINTENANCE	**$250–$500**
	This will vary based not only on location but also on size of roof, roof material, and complexity of the roof.
ROOF SHEATHING	**$40–$50 per sheet (4' × 8' sheets)**
	Roofers will replace entire sheets of sheathing, even if only a fraction of a piece is damaged. So, expect to pay for sheathing repairs based on the number of sheets of wood that are needed.
ROOF REPLACEMENT	**Asphalt shingles: $180-$350 per square.**
	Wood shingles: $450-$700 per square.
	Steel roof: $350-$900 per square.
	Aluminum roof: $750-$1,000 per square.
	Slate roof: $1,000-$3,000 per square.
	Asphalt shingle is by far the most common roofing material, and to give you an idea of the labor versus material breakdown for this type of roof, you should expect that the materials portion of the cost will range from $100 to $150 per square. The rest will go to labor.
	For extra layers of shingles that must be torn off and disposed of, multiply the price by an extra 30 percent for each additional layer.
	You'll notice that there are some very large price ranges above. While I try to keep the ranges small for most of the tasks in this book, roofing is one area where there is tremendous variation in material and labor cost.

1

ROOF REPLACEMENT (CONT'D)

For materials, the cost variation is largely due to climate variation. In cold climates, roofing requirements need to handle extreme temperatures and snow accumulation. This adds cost for additional and more durable materials.

In terms of labor, roofing has one of the highest insurance costs. In locations where insurance is expensive or where you're hiring union contractors, roofing will tend to be much costlier than in locations where insurance is less expensive, and you are using non-union contractors.

While we always recommend using insured contractors for rehab work, roofing is one area where the cost between insured and uninsured contractors will be substantial. (That said, to avoid the significant liability exposure you'll face if an uninsured roofer were to fall off or a roof and injure or kill himself, I *always* recommend using insured roofing professionals. If you're in doubt about your roofer's insurance status, don't hesitate to ask him to provide proof of insurance.)

Other things that drive these large price ranges and will affect the cost of replacement include the complexity of the roof, the height of the property, and the time of year, which can affect weather conditions and temperature.

Determining Your Local Prices

Determining the cost of roofing work in your area shouldn't be very difficult. Most roofing contractors are willing to provide price guidelines without coming out to see a property, assuming you can adequately describe the job. My recommendation is to call several roofing contractors and ask them, "As a ballpark estimate, how much do you charge per square to remove, haul away, and replace a typical, non-complex, 20-square roof on a two-story property?" Make sure you verify that the price they give you includes labor, materials, and dumpster.

You'll likely get a diverse range of answers. Some roofers may insist on coming out to the property before giving a response, in which case they are likely either using that as a sales tactic or they are high end and believe they'll need to convince you in person that they are your roofer of choice.

Generally speaking, they *won't* be your roofer of choice.

In terms of where to find roofing contractors, I would highly recommend asking other investors in your area, or perhaps checking with your local Real Estate Investors Association (REIA). Because there is such a wide range of pricing for roofing, and lots of upsell on features like lifetime warranty, it's easy to overpay on roof work. Roofers who are accustomed to working with investors generally provide the best combination of quality work and reasonable prices.

How to Pay for the Job

Roofing is one of the few renovation areas where the materials required at the beginning of the job can comprise a significant portion of the total cost of work. While I very much prefer working with roofers who can front the cost of the materials and don't charge until the job is completed, I will occasionally work with roofers who insist on material payment upfront.

When this is the case, I will generally agree to pay for materials at the time they are delivered to the jobsite, which is generally the night before or the morning of the start of work. I will never pay more than 50 percent of the total cost of the job upfront (after the materials are delivered) and I will not pay the remaining amount until the satisfactory completion of the job.

Typically, tearing off and replacing a standard roof can be completed in one or two days, so there is little reason for intermediate payment between the time the materials are purchased and the job is completed.

COMPONENT #2
GUTTERS, SOFFIT, AND FASCIA

Overview

The soffit and fascia make up the architectural component beneath the edge of the overhanging roof running around the house. The fascia board is the trim piece that you see beneath the roof, covering the otherwise exposed ends of the roof rafters. The soffit is the covering beneath the fascia that runs parallel to the ground. If you stand under your roof's overhang and look up, you'll be staring at the soffit. Some rustic buildings don't have soffits, and if that's the case you'll be looking up at the roof rafters, between which you'll likely find wasp's nests or other cozy insect shelters.

The soffit and fascia provide an aesthetic component to the house, provide a weather-barrier from the underside of the roof and attic, and often provide ventilation to the entire roof structure. The other purpose of fascia board is to provide a place to attach the gutters.

Fascia board is often made of wood (OSB, plywood, or pine) and soffits are generally made of wood or vinyl. It's not uncommon to have the fascia boards "wrapped" with vinyl or aluminum, both for aesthetic reasons and to provide a better moisture barrier. This work is often done when the siding is vinyl or aluminum and the homeowner wants the trim to match in color and style.

The sole purpose of gutters is to move rainwater away from your house. While there are lots of gutter materials and styles, there are generally two components: the horizontal gutters that sit below your roof to capture water as it streams down; and the vertical downspouts that take water from the horizontal gutters, down the length of the house, and hopefully several feet from the house's foundation once it gets to the ground.

Gutters can be made from one of several materials:

- **Aluminum:** This is the most popular gutter material. Aluminum gutters are lightweight, resistant to rust, and easy to cut (for those installing it). It's also the cheapest of the popular gutter materials. On the downside, aluminum is weaker than the other materials, so leaning a ladder against the gutters or a falling tree branch can easily cause damage. Aluminum is also more susceptible to weather changes; the expansion and contraction during hot and cold weather can cause gutters to pull away from the fascia board and leak.

- **Steel:** Galvanized 24- and 26-gauge steel is the next most popular choice for gutters. Steel is more expensive than aluminum but is high strength and less susceptible to damage. Steel is also heavier—about the twice the weight of aluminum—making installation more difficult. But the big upside to steel gutters is the fact that they will last much longer than aluminum, making long-term upkeep much easier.

- **Vinyl or plastic:** These gutters are by far the cheapest materials but are only good in locations where the weather is temperate, and it doesn't get very cold or hot. Hot and cold weather will cause the vinyl or plastic gutters to expand and contract, making them brittle and conducive to cracking. If you live in an area where vinyl or plastic gutters are common, you may be able to save some money, but be careful to ensure that these gutters are appropriate for your house and location.

- **Copper or zinc:** These are the Rolls-Royce of gutters, with a cost up to three or four times that of aluminum or steel. These types of gutters are mostly used on high-end homes and reconstruction of historic homes to adhere to original detail. It's very unlikely you'll ever be using these materials on a rehab property, so I'll leave it at that.

In addition to the various gutter materials, there are many different styles of gutter. For the most part, the purpose of different gutter styles is purely aesthetic, though one style of gutter has become very prominent over the past 30 years. "Seamless gutters" are made onsite; the installer starts with a long strip of metal that rolls through a machine that creates the gutter of the exact length required. The advantages are obvious—quick production, the aesthetic value of no seams, and faster installation.

While you can still buy gutters in pre-cut lengths ("sectional" gutters), these make up a very small percentage of the overall market and are usually used when building high-end custom houses with the more exotic metal choices such as zinc or copper.

The other major consideration when buying gutters is whether to buy "gutter guards" or install covers over the gutters. If the house is on a wooded lot where lots of leaves or debris will likely be falling into the gutters, installing covers over the gutters will make maintenance much easier and will help extend the life of the gutters.

Gutters generally come in a variety of colors (especially aluminum), a variety of sizes, various thicknesses, and with different coatings. Your location will often help determine the specific type of gutter you'll use, but pricing is pretty consistent within a particular material choice.

Inspection Tips

Repairing gutters, soffits, and fascia is relatively inexpensive, but repairing the damage that can be caused by old or defective components can be costly. Especially with gutters, it's important to catch issues before they result in siding, attic, or interior wall problems. Taking a few extra moments upfront to examine the gutter system can save you headaches and money later on.

When inspecting the gutters, the first thing to look for is that they are continuous, without any breaks, and that they slope towards the downspouts. If there is excessive debris in the gutters, but no obvious source of the debris (e.g., no overhanging tree branches), this can be an indication that the gutters are sloped inappropriately, and water is not flowing to the downspouts and away from the house.

The next thing you should be looking for with respect to the gutters is any sign of leakage. When water leaks from the gutters, you run the risk of water intrusion through the exterior walls, as well as pooling of water near the foundation, which can lead to a wet basement.

To determine if gutters are leaking, here are a few things to look for:
- Rust on the bottom or house-facing sides of the gutters;
- Gaps in gutter seams;
- Stains or discoloration on fascia board or siding behind or below the gutters.

Finally, you should ensure that downspouts either terminate at least several feet from the foundation or at a splashblock (a sloped block at the bottom of the downspout) that leads water away from the house. If downspouts are missing, or if they terminate against the foundation wall, you may find indications of water intrusion through the foundation and into the crawlspace or basement. In many cases, fixing gutters and correcting downspouts is enough to remediate a wet basement or crawlspace.

For the soffit and fascia, assuming you can't get close enough to inspect them directly, I recommend looking for any signs of obvious rot, including chipping paint or discoloration from moisture. It can be difficult to determine the condition of soffit and fascia from the ground, but a good roofer will include a soffit and fascia inspection as part of a roof inspection or basic roof maintenance.

Life Expectancy

Soffit and fascia: Depending on the materials used, every soffit and fascia should last 20 or more years without rotting, decaying, or deteriorating. Oftentimes, fascia board will be the first place that requires repainting, but don't confuse chipping or peeling paint with actual damage—oftentimes you'll find that there is no damage beneath the paint.

Gutters: If well maintained (cleaned at least several times per year), gutters should last about 20 to 30 years. Typically, professional gutter installers will provide up to a 20-year warranty.

Scope of Work (SOW) Tasks

When it comes to gutters, unless the gutters just need to be cleaned or reattached to the fascia board, there generally isn't much in the way of maintenance. The bulk of the work you end up doing on gutters will be replacing them when they are missing, damaged, rusted, or leaking. Because you can generally paint new gutters to match the old ones, you can replace either small or large sections without too much difficulty.

CLEAN GUTTERS	Cleaning gutters involves either removing debris by hand or using a leaf blower or similar device to blow debris out of the gutters. If there's a lot of built-up debris, it may be necessary to remove downspouts to clean them, and then reattach after they are cleaned. Work will generally be done by a roofing company or a company specializing in gutter repair and replacement, though there are freelance contractors out there who will clean gutters at a reasonable price. Just ensure that they are properly insured, as gutter cleaning can be dangerous, especially on tall or highly pitched roofs.

REPLACE GUTTERS	Gutters can be replaced in small or large sections to match existing gutters or can be replaced completely. Gutters and downspouts are usually measured and priced per linear foot.
	Work will generally be done by a roofing company or a company that specializes in gutter repair and replacement.
REPLACE SOFFIT AND FASCIA	Soffit and fascia can be replaced in small or large sections but will often require gutters to be disconnected prior to repair, and to inspect behind them for additional damage.
	Work can be done by a qualified carpenter, a roofing company, or a company specializing in gutter repair and replacement.

Cost Guidelines

Here are the typical costs associated with gutter work:

CLEAN GUTTERS	**$100-$300**
	The cost to clean gutters will generally depend on three things:
	1. The total amount of gutters (linear feet).
	2. The height and steepness of the roof.
	3. Whether downspouts need to be detached to be cleaned.
REPLACE GUTTERS	**Aluminum: $4-$8 per linear foot of gutter or downspout.**
	Steel: $4-$8 per linear foot of gutter or downspout.
	Vinyl/plastic: $3-$5 per linear foot of gutter or downspout.
	Copper/zinc: $15-$30 per linear foot of gutter or downspout.
	Gutters are measured and priced per linear foot. Replacement is generally quoted for labor and materials combined.

REPLACE SOFFIT AND FASCIA	Wood: $5-$10 per linear foot of soffit and fascia.
	Vinyl: $6-$12 per linear foot of soffit and fascia.
	Aluminum: $8-$15 per linear foot of soffit and fascia.
	Soffit and fascia are measured and priced per linear foot. Replacement is generally quoted for labor and materials combined.

Determining Your Local Prices

Gutters will generally be provided and installed by either a roofing contractor or a siding contractor, though there are a few companies that specialize in gutter installation only. Once you determine the gutter material you wish to use, prices can generally be determined with phone calls to various roofing and siding contractors, asking for their price per linear foot, including both labor and materials.

Generally speaking, if you're doing any roofing or siding work on the house, you should try to use the same contractors for the gutters, as you'll get better pricing that way. Also note that gutters are one of those renovation items where the contractor is likely accustomed to working with retail homeowners and the initial price you get will likely be much higher than what you can negotiate to.

How to Pay for the Job

Because gutter installation (or cleaning) is generally a one-day job, and materials aren't a huge upfront cost, I would recommend paying for all gutter work once the job is complete.

COMPONENT #3
SIDING

Overview

There are several layers of material that form the exterior of the house, and these layers serve several purposes: weatherproof the interior, allow moisture to pass through the walls, and provide an aesthetic finish to the exterior of the house. In some cases, most commonly masonry brick and stone siding, this component will also figure into the structure of the house. But in most cases, the structure of the house consists of wood framing, and none of the siding components—including brick and stone—are structural.

In general, the siding layers will consist of three components:

- Sheathing
- House wrap
- Siding

SHEATHING

The sheathing is the layer closest to the interior of the house and is attached directly to the framing studs. In some cases, the sheathing is structural, while in other cases it's just an extra layer of barrier and insulation. Common sheathing material includes plywood, wafer-board, OSB, or even rigid insulation in newer and more upscale houses. In older houses, you'll see that the sheathing is just wooden boards nailed to the studs.

Unless you're building an addition or have some major wall deterioration due to moisture or termites, you probably won't have to replace much sheathing on a typical renovation. If you do, it's best to just match the existing sheathing currently used around the rest of the structure.

HOUSE WRAP

The house wrap is the layer that sits between the sheathing and siding and has the primary purpose of being a weather-resistant barrier. House wrap should keep moisture (like rain) from permeating the interior of the structure but should also allow water vapor to pass from the interior to the exterior of the structure. Basically, house wrap keeps moisture from building up in the interior wall cavities.

Historically, this was accomplished by covering the wooden sheathing with tar or tar paper, and more recently asphalt-treated paper. These days, house wrap is either traditional asphalt-treated paper or fiberglass, or one of many synthetic materials designed specifically for this purpose. Tyvek is the most common brand name for house wrap, and if you've been around new construction at all, you probably recognize the name. You will probably only be replacing house wrap when you're replacing or adding sheathing to the house.

3

SIDING

The siding or cladding is the layer that is seen from the exterior of the house. It acts as a weather barrier and provides a nice aesthetic look to the house. There are lots of different materials that can (and have) been used to side houses, with the most common being:

- **Wood:** Wood is the oldest style of siding material around. It requires more upkeep than most other sidings and can be susceptible to rot, termites, and a host of other deteriorating factors. Clapboard wood siding (overlapping boards running horizontally) is historically the most common type of wood siding, but T1-11 (basically just plywood notched for aesthetics) was common in the later parts of the 20th century as well. Wood shingles or cedar "shake" was common in the Northeast and is still used as replacement siding or for aesthetic touches on many houses.

  If you'll be making siding repairs to a house with wood siding, try to match the siding as best you can. If you need to replace large sections of wood siding, I would suggest that you consider residing the entire house in a different material instead. New siding is a great selling feature, and old, deteriorating wood siding is not very attractive, even when painted.

- **Aluminum:** Aluminum siding came next after wood siding and is still used in parts of the country. It's low maintenance and durable, but it's also prone to denting and fading, and can be noisy during rain or windstorms.

  Aluminum siding can be difficult to retrofit, as matching faded colors is nearly impossible. While you can paint aluminum siding, the type of paint required is expensive and if you have major aluminum repairs, you may want to consider just residing the entire house in another siding material instead.

- **Vinyl:** Vinyl siding has been very popular for the past several decades, as it is low cost, low maintenance, and easy to install. On the downside, vinyl siding can be prone to cracking and fading, and is expensive to paint. It can also buckle in extreme heat, or if your barbeque grill is too close to the house.

Vinyl siding is often a good choice when residing a lower- to mid-range house, and it comes in a wide array of colors, so painting is not necessary. When doing vinyl siding repairs, the siding can be very difficult to match due to fading, so in many cases, the siding contractor will replace damaged siding with other siding around the house and install the new siding in less conspicuous places where the replacement is less noticeable.

- **Cement composite:** Cement board siding is relatively new to the market and is a very popular choice for new construction or residing projects. It is very durable, low maintenance, and is considered "green," as it's made mostly from recycled materials. Hardiplank is a common brand name for cement board siding.

  Cement board can emulate most natural wood grain sidings, installs like wood siding, and is cut like wood siding. Because it comes in many different designs and styles and is designed to be painted, it's a great siding material to use to patch existing wood siding—once it's painted, it's difficult to tell which is wood and which is cement board. Cement board siding is relatively expensive, but a great choice when residing a mid- to high-end house.

- **Masonry (brick and stone):** Brick and stone siding can provide a classy touch to a house's exterior, though repairs can be expensive, when necessary. In older brick houses, the brick may be part of the structure of the house, but in many cases, the brick is just a veneer placed in front of the wood framing to provide a specific aesthetic look. You can generally differentiate structural brick from brick veneer by looking closely at the brick. Structural brick will have layers of "header brick"—brick that is turned sideways (you only see the short end). Structural brick will also have brick arches over windows and other openings for structural integrity. Brick veneer will have holes—called "weep holes"—placed every few feet along the bottom layer of bricks.

  When doing any work on structural brick, you'll likely want to get a review by a structural engineer before starting and you'll most certainly want to use an experienced and qualified mason. When repairing or replacing brick or stone veneers, I recommend that you use an experienced mason, though many carpenters can do very minor brickwork or repointing without much trouble.

When doing siding repair and replacement, oftentimes the biggest challenge will be to match existing siding with replacement materials. A good carpenter or siding contractor will have experience matching siding, using trim to hide transitions, using paint to obscure material differences, or moving siding pieces around to make the siding look uniform. But if you find that too much of the siding needs to be replaced, or that matching existing siding just isn't feasible, your best options are generally either to replace all of the siding on the house or to break the house into sections, keeping existing siding on certain sections, and replacing the siding on another section. If you do this, make sure you bring in a designer who can help ensure the siding maintains good aesthetics and the different sidings don't clash.

Just like in the roofing industry, large siding replacement jobs are generally measured in squares (a 10' × 10' section, or 100 square feet). Smaller jobs are going to be measured by the square foot, and the cost will mostly be based on the amount of time the contractor expects to spend on the job. In general, I prefer my contractors to provide all material for siding jobs, as transportation of siding can be cumbersome and difficult.

Inspection Tips

Siding is the foremost barrier between the exterior elements and your house. A well-constructed barrier will protect your investment, while a defective exterior barrier can cause ongoing headaches and expense. For this reason, any siding issues should be identified early and addressed quickly.

While siding issues are typically pretty obvious, there are some specific things you should be looking for as you walk the exterior of a property:

- For houses with wood siding, take special note of locations where water can accumulate—for example, near the ground (siding should *never* be touching the ground), above door frames, and below gutters and soffits. This is where you're most likely to find rotted wood that needs to be repaired or replaced.
- For houses with vinyl siding, if you can find a location where it's possible to peek behind the siding, you should check to ensure that there is house wrap between the siding and the sheathing. Vinyl siding is not

watertight, so it should be installed over a barrier that is watertight. If there is no barrier between the vinyl siding and the house sheathing, expect this to come up on your future buyer's inspection report.

- For vinyl siding, also take note of any impact damage. Vinyl siding can easily be damaged by hail, baseballs, and other things that hit the siding on a daily basis. While replacing damaged siding is not difficult or expensive, one issue you might run into is that older siding is often faded from sun exposure, so new siding will not match well and will stand out. One of the tricks that good vinyl siding contractors will use is that they'll move older siding from less conspicuous places—like the back of the house—to repair the older siding, and then install the new siding in the less conspicuous location.

- For cement board siding, the most common issue is improper installation and nails that are either not inserted deep enough or inserted too deep ("countersunk"). If the nails are not snug to the siding, this can be an opportunity for water to intrude into the nail holes, which can cause damage to sheathing and interior walls. For cement board siding, I always recommend being familiar with the installation instructions for the specific brand that is used, and to walk the house to verify that the instructions were followed.

- For hard siding surfaces including brick, stucco, and stone, identifying issues can be difficult. Water intrusion is generally not obvious from the exterior, and by the time it's apparent from the interior, there could already be substantial damage. When inspecting hard siding surfaces such as these, look for areas of missing mortar (in the case of brick or stone) and take careful note of areas directly between window sills and gutters—two places where a lot of water tends to hit.

Life Expectancy
Different siding materials generally have differing life expectancies:
- Wood: 20-30 years.
- Aluminum: 20-30 years.
- Vinyl: 20-40 years.
- Cement composite: 40+ years.
- Masonry: 100+ years.

Scope of Work (SOW) Tasks

The following are the basic SOW tasks associated with siding work:

PRESSURE WASHING	Over time, siding will pick up dirt, algae, and mold, and oftentimes a good pressure washing of the exterior of the house will make a huge difference in appearance. In fact, for many newer homes, I will pressure wash before I decide whether to repaint, as pressure washing can sometimes provide enough restoration of the exterior that painting isn't necessary. Pressure washing is especially helpful when dealing with vinyl or aluminum sidings, as they are generally not painted and can pick up a moldy film that makes the siding appear to be in worse condition than it actually is.
REMOVE OLD SIDING	If you'll be doing a major siding replacement, don't forget to factor in the cost of removing and disposing of old siding.
REPLACE SHEATHING	If you'll be doing any major siding work, or will be doing an addition, you'll likely have some sheathing that needs to be added or replaced. Whichever of your contractors is doing your siding repair should have the knowledge and ability to replace sheathing when and where necessary.
REPLACE HOUSE WRAP	If you'll be doing any major siding work, or will be doing an addition, you'll likely have some house wrap that needs to be added or replaced. Whichever of your contractors is doing your siding repair should have the knowledge and ability to replace house wrap when and where necessary.

PATCH SIDING	For small siding repairs, your painters or carpenters may be able to do the work more inexpensively than hiring a siding company. I will generally have my exterior painters do small siding repairs as part of their painting preparation, and because they are working on the exterior of the house anyway, they will generally do this work at a very reasonable price. Of course, you want to verify that whoever is doing your siding repairs is qualified, as poor siding installation can seriously detract from the aesthetic value of the house.
REPLACE SIDING	If the amount of siding repair is significant, or if the siding on your house doesn't measure up to surrounding or competing properties, you may want to consider residing the whole house. While expensive, new siding is a great selling point and can give your house tremendous curb appeal.

Cost Guidelines

Siding costs will vary tremendously by area, as materials prices are inconsistent around the country. Labor costs also tend to vary a lot by location, as weather conditions will greatly impact the time and effort required to deal with siding issues:

PRESSURE WASH	$200-$500 for whole house
REMOVE OLD SIDING	$50-$100 per square
REPLACE SHEATHING	$40-$50 per sheet Most sheathing on low- to mid-end houses will be OSB or plywood that comes in 4' × 8' sheets. Typical material prices run about $.35 to $.50 per square foot and typical installation prices run about twice the materials cost.
REPLACE HOUSE WRAP	$300-$600 for whole house

PATCH SIDING	**$3-$6 per square foot**
	Patching siding is going to consist of purchasing the materials and a labor price that will likely be related to the amount of time the contractor spends working on the repairs. This price is just an average for most types of siding material, but keep in mind that more expensive materials will push the price to the higher end. Also note that the same size repair to an easily accessible part of the house could be a lot more expensive if it has to be done on a very difficult to reach part of the house, as the time and risk are increased.
REPLACE SIDING	**Wood: $400-$700 per square.**
	Aluminum: $200-$350 per square.
	Vinyl: $150-$350 per square.
	Cement board: $300-$600 per square.
	Masonry: $15-$25 per square foot.
	Siding costs will vary by both location and siding material. Colder climates generally require better insulated siding materials, which typically cost more. In addition, most siding lines will have different levels of quality within each material. For example, low-end vinyl siding is much less expensive than high-end vinyl with an insulated backing.
	Additionally, if you choose a siding material that isn't common for your area, both material and labor costs will be significantly higher than using a common material in your area.

Determining Your Local Prices

Many siding contractors will be willing to give you ballpark estimates on siding replacement. For smaller siding jobs, you'll likely need to have your contractor look at the work before determining a price, as the labor cost will ultimately be determined by the amount of time the contractor expects to spend.

How to Pay for the Job

For large jobs, I'll generally expect to pay for the siding material upfront, just before the job starts. The remainder of the cost will be paid at the completion of the job.

COMPONENT #4
EXTERIOR PAINTING

Overview

Exterior painting (including staining for wood components) is pretty straightforward—it covers the painting of any or all of the following exterior components of the property:

- Siding.
- Trim.
- Exterior doors and shutters.
- Decks.

When an entire exterior is painted, it is most common for the paint scheme to involve three colors—one for the siding, one for the trim, and one for the doors and shutters. This three-color paint scheme is fairly typical these days. Wood decks and porches will generally be painted or stained a color that matches one of the other three that is used.

The cost of painting these components will vary based on several factors:

- Prep work required.
- Size of job (square footage).
- Number of coats of paint.
- Complexity of job (intricacy of detail).
- Difficulty of job (heights or difficult to reach locations).
- Type of paint required.

The most commonly ignored variable in the list above is the prep work—the amount of preparation required prior to painting can double the cost of the job. Preparation may involve things like pressure washing, caulking siding joints and seams, scraping old paint, or caulking nail holes. This is work that may or may not be done by your siding crew, so be sure to determine who will do this prep work and don't end up paying double for it.

Here are some very general figures that will factor into exterior paint pricing. Don't use this as a direct pricing formula, but this should help you get your head around where the costs are coming from:

- A typical mid-grade quality paint will cost about $20-$40 per gallon.
- For a typical investor-quality painter, materials will run about 20 percent of the total cost of the project.
- Prep work will generally add between 50 percent and 150 percent of the cost of the project, depending on how much work is needed prior to painting.
- Painting trim will generally cost about 50 percent more than painting siding, as the work is more intricate.
- Hand brushing will generally add 25 percent or more to the cost versus spraying but will result in a much longer-lasting paint finish.
- Generally, one coat of paint is enough for the exterior, but if you're going from a very dark to a very light color, or vice-versa, you may need two coats of paint or a coat of primer prior to painting. An extra coat of paint will generally add about 25 percent or more to the cost.
- Prices are generally lower between October and March when fewer people are thinking about getting their houses painted and painters need more work.

4

One last thing to keep in mind is that exterior paint is exposed to the elements and will quickly fade and stain. Therefore, it's very difficult to just touch-up exterior paint or paint individual sections, as the new paint will not likely match the old paint.

Inspection Tips

The condition of exterior paint should be obvious. Signs of paint chipping, major discoloration, or areas of siding where paint has been stripped away are indications that the exterior should be pressure-washed and repainted.

Life Expectancy

A good exterior paint job may start to fade after seven to ten years, and color tastes generally change every ten to 20 years as well. If you buy a house that hasn't been painted in ten years or more, you should seriously consider repainting; if you have a house that hasn't been painted in 15 years or more, you *definitely* should consider repainting. Trim generally will need repainting sooner than siding, so if you're trying to save money and the paint is in mostly good condition, you may be able to get away with just repainting the trim, doors, and shutters.

Scope of Work (SOW) Tasks

Exterior painting isn't rocket science. You should be able to take a quick walk around the exterior of the property to determine if the house needs to be repainted, either completely or in sections. Here are the typical SOW tasks associated with exterior painting:

PAINT EXTERIOR	If a house hasn't been painted in more than 15 years, or if the paint is outdated or in bad shape, you'll likely want to repaint the entire exterior, including siding, trim, doors, and shutters.
PAINT TRIM ONLY	If the exterior paint on the body of the house is in relatively good shape, you can often get away with just painting the trim, and perhaps repainting exterior doors and shutters.

Cost Guidelines

With painting, you have the choice of getting either labor-only or labor-and-materials bids. Because good painters can generally get better discounts on materials than I can, and because buying and hauling around a lot of paint isn't easy work, I much prefer to get combined labor-and-materials bids on jobs. My costs below will reflect both labor and material, though you are welcome to break out your costs based on the material cost information I provided earlier in this section.

Here are the cost guidelines associated with the exterior painting tasks above:

PAINT EXTERIOR	**$1.50-$3.00 per square foot of above ground interior floor space.**
	Note that the cost of paint has increased significantly over the past several years, which has driven up the cost of both interior and exterior painting.
	While I could give you more precise formulas for estimating exterior paint costs, the time and effort it would take wouldn't be worth the trouble.
	For a typical 1- or 2-story house between 1,000 and 3,000 square feet, requiring basic prep work (pressure washing, some caulking), one coat of mid-grade exterior paint, hand-brushing the trim, and spraying the siding, you should expect to pay from $1.50 to $3.00 per square foot of interior space.
	For my typical 2-story, 1,500-square-foot traditional houses, I generally pay about $2,500 for prep and painting of siding, trim, doors, and shutters.
PAINT TRIM ONLY	**$.50-$1.00 per square foot of interior floor space**
	Because trim painting is more detailed, generally requires more prep work, typically is done by brush, and is often located in taller and harder to reach areas, the cost of painting just the trim is often a decent percentage of the entire cost of the project.
	This is why I will paint an entire house instead of just the trim—the total price only increases about $1,200–$1,500, but the impact of a fully, newly painted house is much more substantial.

4

Determining Your Local Prices

Getting bids for exterior paint is generally very easy. Because the work is on the exterior of the house, you generally don't even need to be onsite when the contractor comes to see the job. This is why I will call several painters, give them the address of the house, and let them know that they are welcome to stop by and take a look at their convenience. This way, I can get many bids with minimal time and effort on my part.

Once I have narrowed down the painters based on their bids, I'll meet with them to walk through the interior of the house and get interior pricing as well. I will typically hire one painting crew to paint both interior and exterior of the house, so this will be my opportunity to "interview" them and decide if they will be getting the entire job or none of it.

How to Pay for the Job

I like to pay for the painting at the completion of the work but will make some exceptions. If a painter is doing both the interior and exterior of the house, I will gladly pay for either the interior or the exterior when that part of the job is complete and then pay for the other half when that part of the job is complete.

On some occasions, a painter will ask for a deposit or for payment of materials upfront. If I have worked with the painter in the past, I may consider paying 30 percent upfront (which should cover material costs), or better yet, I may consider paying the paint supplier directly for the actual paint purchased.

Never pay more than 30 percent upfront for painting, as this will generally exceed the cost of materials necessary for the job.

COMPONENT #5
DECKS AND PORCHES

Overview

In this section, we'll consider the work and cost associated with building standard wood decks and porches. Like many other parts of the renovation, the exact specifications of the work are going to determine the pricing, but I will discuss what you should expect in terms of building a basic no-frills structure with standard lower-end materials.

For the purpose of defining and estimating the cost to construct, a deck consists of three main components:

- Framing
- Decking
- Railings

FRAMING

The framing is the structure of the deck consisting of the ledger board (the piece of the deck that attaches to the side of the house), the front rim joist (the board parallel to the house at the front of the deck), the side rim joists (the boards on the sides of the deck perpendicular to the house), the interior joists, and the posts/footers that support the deck. For this discussion, we're going to assume the deck is within a few feet of the ground, and that only two or three posts and footers are needed at the front of the deck.

DECKING

The decking is the top layer of the deck—the material that you see and walk on. While pressure-treated wood is standard for decking, there are many exotic woods as well as synthetic materials you can use.

In fact, synthetic materials have become a lot more popular over the past decade, simply because of their aesthetic appeal and the fact that they will last much longer than traditional wood decking.

RAILINGS

For the railings around the deck, the three major components are the railings, the balusters (spindles), and the posts. Like decking material, you have lots of wood and synthetic material choices, as well as upgrades in railing design and baluster design. For this discussion we'll assume a standard wood railing with plain balusters.

The best way to estimate the cost of a deck is to use a square footage price. Deck materials mostly consist of wood and screws or nails, and those material costs won't vary a tremendous amount among geographic areas. Labor prices will vary based on area, and also based on the skill of the contractor(s) doing the work.

Unless you're doing a high-end rehab or a complex deck project, you probably don't want to use a professional deck builder, as the costs will be much higher than just finding a skilled carpenter. Also, keep in mind that while decks are generally not very difficult to build, you'll probably want to find a carpenter who excels at finish work. Things like the design of the railings and balusters, the symmetry of the posts, and other aesthetic factors make a big difference in the appeal of the finished product.

Make sure you discuss with your deck builder who will provide the materials. While it's not overly difficult to estimate the materials you need for the job, transporting deck materials (10'+ lengths of lumber) can be cumbersome. If you get the materials delivered and you order too much, you need to figure out how to get the extra stuff back to the store; if you order too little, you need to pay for a second delivery. For these reasons, I prefer a fixed price bid that includes the contractor purchasing materials.

Inspection Tips

I don't have enough space in this book to do a detailed discussion of all the codes and engineering best practices associated with building decks and porches, but I do want to give you some red flags to look for that can indicate an improperly constructed deck or porch. Keep in mind that a poorly constructed deck can lead to severe injury or even death. So, if you have *any* concerns about the construction of a deck on one of your properties—and especially if the deck is more than a few feet off the ground—bring in a qualified contractor or engineer to do an examination.

With that in mind, here are some things you should be looking for when inspecting a wooden deck or porch:

- Typically speaking, decks need to carry an evenly disbursed load over the entire deck, which means that about 50 percent of the load will need to be supported by the deck connection to the house and about 50 percent of the load will need to be supported by the posts at the far end of the deck. For this reason, you should be focusing your inspection equally on both sides of the deck—and everything in between.

- The posts should sit on concrete footers that are poured below the frost line (the minimum depth in the ground below which the soil doesn't freeze). For example, if the frost line in your area is 24" (this can generally be found in local codes), the top of the concrete footer on which your deck post sits should be at least 24" underground.

- Deck posts should be *attached* to the footers on which they sit, not just resting on the footers. This is to prevent the posts from slipping or shifting off the footers. The most common type of attachment is a steel plate that rests on top of the footer and is bolted to the deck post.

- Deck posts that are at least 6" × 6" should be large enough to support any deck less than 12 feet in height. While 4" × 4" deck posts are often large enough to accommodate smaller decks, if you have any questions about whether the size of the deck posts is sufficient to support the deck, bring in an engineer or experienced contractor.

- Any piece of structural support for the deck that is installed within 18" of the ground should be composed of treated wood. This includes the deck posts and any joists under or around the deck. Untreated wood will rot when exposed to prolonged moisture, which will eventually cause the structure to become unsound.

- The ledger board attached to the house will need to support 50 percent of the deck load, so it's important to ensure that the ledger board is correctly attached to the house. The correct way to attach the ledger board is to use lag bolts or through bolts, which are extremely strong and thick bolts that go all the way through both the ledger board and the rim joist of the house. (The rim joist is part of the exterior wall construction and is what holds the flooring system of the house together.) It can be difficult to determine if the ledger board is correctly attached to the house, so if you have any doubts, bring in an expert to verify.

Even if you determine that everything I've noted above has been done correctly on the deck, that doesn't mean the deck is sound or up to local codes. Structural design of a deck can be complicated, and I always recommend that you bring in an expert—an engineer or qualified contractor—to verify that any decks or porches are structurally sound.

Life Expectancy

Thirty to 50 years, depending on materials used.

Scope of Work (SOW) Tasks

While there are endless deck and porch designs, each of which can be accomplished with dozens of materials and building techniques, I'm going to limit my SOW tasks to just the building of a basic deck:

5

BUILD DECK	This consists of building a basic house-attached, pressure-treated wood deck within a few feet of the ground, with basic railings and balusters, and a step or two down from the deck to the ground.

Cost Guidelines

The three biggest components to deck cost are size, materials, and intricacy. Per-foot prices can increase quickly when designs get intricate, expensive materials are used, or multiple levels are added. Standard no-frills decks made out of basic wood materials are pretty consistent in their pricing:

BUILD DECK	**$18-$30 per square foot.**
	The materials for wood decks will generally run about $8-$10 per square foot. Labor prices will generally run about $10-$20 per square foot for a qualified carpenter.
	The above pricing assumes a wood decking, which costs about $1.50-$2.00 per square foot. If you choose to use synthetic materials for your decking, you can expect to add another $1.50-$5.00 per square foot of decking.
	For example, a 10' × 10' deck with wood decking boards might cost $2,500 to build; that same deck with synthetic decking boards would likely increase in price to between $2,650 and $3,000, depending on the specific decking material used.

Determining Your Local Prices

While many carpenters will want to know specifics before quoting you a deck price, you can generally convince them to give you an idea of what they would charge per square foot by asking what they'd charge for a basic 10' × 10' deck, and then dividing that price by 100.

How to Pay for the Job

Expect to pay for materials upfront (and perhaps provide materials) and labor upon completion.

5

COMPONENT #6
CONCRETE

Overview

Concrete is a mixture of cement, sand, gravel, and water. You can buy concrete either pre-mixed in liquid form, delivered via cement mixer truck and poured in large quantities directly where you want it, or in dry form—up to 80-pound bags—from the big-box stores. Delivery of pre-mixed concrete is great for poured foundations and large driveways but isn't nearly as convenient as mixing small quantities of dry concrete with water at your own convenience.

There are lots of different types of concrete work you may need to do on a renovation, from little stuff (repair cracks, pour deck footers, build steps) to large jobs (pour a new foundation, replace a sidewalk, build a driveway or porch) and everything in between.

While some cement tasks consist of the basic concrete material and the labor to apply and mold the concrete, other jobs involve a lot of associated tasks. For example, pouring a new concrete driveway, while a big concrete project, also involves excavation, laying of sand and gravel, and creating molds. So, while it may be easy to determine the labor and materials pricing for the concrete portion of the job, you'll often need to consider other related tasks and materials as well.

Because there are so many variations on concrete work, from the very big jobs of pouring a foundation, building a porch, or installing a driveway, to the small jobs including fixing cracks in a sidewalk or installing a deck footer, I just can't cover every concrete task in this section. But I do want to provide some general pricing guidelines for both large and small concrete jobs.

For large jobs, you'll buy concrete from a supplier who will deliver and pour the liquid concrete from their cement truck. Concrete is purchased by the cubic yard. For small jobs, you'll buy bags of dry concrete from the big-box stores, mix it with water in batch sizes as needed, and use at your convenience. For medium sized projects, many concrete contractors will have a portable cement mixer that can hold several bags of dry concrete mix and water. This will allow you to do large concrete jobs without the overhead of having the concrete delivered by truck.

Inspection Tips

There are two types of concrete repairs you'll need to consider on your rehabs:

1. Structural and functional issues. This includes things like cracked or bowing concrete retaining walls, major concrete driveway issues, and concrete steps that have deteriorated or pulled away from a porch or deck.

2. Cosmetic issues. This includes typical concrete issues like cracks, discoloration, and other aesthetic issues can detract from the value of the property.

With any structural or functional issues related to concrete, it's best to bring in an engineer or specialized contractor to evaluate and make a repair recommendation. Any decisions related to fixing cosmetic concrete issues including cracked sidewalks or discolored garage floors should ultimately boil down to the estimated cost of repair versus the impact that repair will have on the ARV or the salability of the house.

6

Life Expectancy

Bag of dry cement: one to two months.

Poured concrete: Driveways will last 30-50 years, while buildings could last 1,000 years or more (like the ones built by ancient Romans!)

Scope of Work (SOW) Tasks

In the section below, I will discuss how the labor and material costs generally break down for both small and large concrete jobs:

LARGE CONCRETE JOBS	Large concrete jobs include things like: • Poured foundation • New driveway • Concrete porch • Concrete steps • Concrete walls
SMALL CONCRETE JOBS	Small concrete jobs include things like: • Repairing cracks • Pouring deck footers • Repairing concrete steps

Cost Guidelines

Here are some very basic costs guidelines for both small and large concrete jobs:

LARGE CONCRETE JOBS	**$5-$10 per square foot.** Liquid concrete generally costs between $100 and $120 per cubic yard (27 cubic feet). Given that a typical concrete pour for a porch or driveway is 4"-6" deep, a yard of concrete will cover between 50-80 square feet of space. That means the concrete costs for a large project will run $1.50-$2.50 per sf. There will be additional material costs in addition to the concrete. Note that the cost of delivering concrete to a jobsite will vary based on the distance from the concrete plant to the site and the amount of concrete you order. If you purchase less than a full truckload of concrete (about 10 cubic yards), you will pay a premium for delivery. Labor costs will depend on the scope of the work. If the job is a simple pour into a location that requires a simple mold, you may be looking at only $3-$4 per square foot. More complicated projects that require excavation, grading, or complex molds could be closer to $8-$10 per square foot.
SMALL CONCRETE JOBS	**$5-$10 per square foot.** An 80-pound bag of dry concrete mix will cost between $3.50 and $5.50 and will cover approximately 0.6 cubic feet. For a project that requires a 4"-6" thick slab of concrete, one bag will cover approximately 1-2 square feet of space. That means the concrete alone costs $1.75-$5.50 per sf. And there may be additional material costs on top of the concrete. For small jobs, labor prices will likely be determined by the amount of time spent completing the work, and a good concrete layer or carpenter will run $25-$35 per hour.

Determining Your Local Prices

For large concrete jobs, you can estimate based on the square footage (for a large estimate range), but you will want to get bids to see what the actual cost will be. This is one area where I would recommend you speak with other investors to get references for good concrete layers in your area. Prices will vary greatly, and if you're paying retail for concrete work, you're going to spend way too much.

For small jobs, you'll likely purchase the concrete yourself and pay your concrete layer (or carpenter) by the hour. It's also quite possible that the concrete work will be part of a larger job (for example, pouring footers for a deck) and the price will be included in the larger job.

How to Pay for the Job

How you pay for the job will depend on what the specific job is and what type of contractor you're working with. If it's a large company, you may be able to pay in installments or when work is complete; if you're working with individual laborers, you may have to purchase materials upfront and pay as you go.

6

COMPONENT #7
GARAGE

Overview

The bulk of the cost of garage work will fall into other renovation components—demo, concrete, framing, sheetrock, painting, doors, or windows. But I consider the garage doors and garage door openers to be a separate component that will need to be evaluated and addressed separately from the rest of the renovation scope.

Standard garage doors come in vinyl, steel, or wood, with steel being by far the most popular. Doors may be insulated or not insulated, may have windows in one or more panels and come in a variety of patterns and designs. Most vinyl and steel doors will last decades if they are used properly and don't sustain any major dents. Wood doors are more expensive but are custom looking and can add value to a higher-end house. They are more susceptible to the elements and are more likely to need to be replaced if you buy an older house with wood doors.

Garage door openers are typically chain-driven, belt-driven, or screw-driven. Chain-drive models use a metal chain to pull the door open on a track. These are the most common and inexpensive type of opener, but also the noisiest. Belt drives use a rubber belt and are virtually silent, but you'll pay more for that advantage. Screw drives use a lifting device that runs along a threaded steel rod; these drives have fewer moving parts, so there is less maintenance required and fewer malfunctions. But these types of openers tend to be less reliable in especially hot or cold climates and are therefore the least common model used in typical single-family houses.

Laws were enacted in 1992 to ensure that all new garage door openers included external sensors and reversing mechanisms to provide safer operation. Openers generally only last ten to 20 years, so it's unlikely that you'll encounter too many houses with openers older than that. But if you do, you should seriously consider replacing the openers, even if they are still in working order.

While you'll probably want to have a professional garage door installer provide the labor and materials for a new door install, you can likely find a good carpenter or handyman to do the opener replacement if you provide the opener yourself. Going this route will likely save you some money.

Inspection Tips

When inspecting a garage, there's a combination of functional, safety, and cosmetic items that you should be evaluating and considering.

In terms of functional concerns:

- You should ensure that the garage door is operational and moves smoothly both opening and closing. You should test functionality from both the garage door remote controls, as well as any controls on the interior or exterior walls of the garage.

In terms of safety issues:

- Should the garage door encounter an object when closing, the opener should automatically reverse direction. Using a hand or knee to block the closing of the door should be enough to get it to reverse and move back to an open position. (Though be careful not to get an arm or leg stuck in a door that isn't operating properly.)
- All new garage door openers should have sensors several inches off the ground that will detect movement under the door and reverse direction should motion be detected while the door is closing.
- If either of the above prove to be issues with your garage door opener, it's worth having the door and its opener evaluated. Improperly functioning doors and openers can pose a significant risk to children and pets, and you can be certain that a good buyer inspector will test this as part of a basic home inspection.
- Any door leading from the interior of the garage to the house should be fire rated. If you're undertaking a significant renovation that requires permits, this may be something a building inspector requires in order to pass inspections.
- Finally, while this may be beyond the scope of your renovation, consider that any attached garage should have at least one step up from the garage floor to the house when entering the house. This is because carbon monoxide—a by-product of car exhaust—is heavier than air and will sink to floor level. By ensuring that there is a step up from garage to house, you mitigate the risk of carbon monoxide flowing from the garage to the interior of the house.

In terms of cosmetic issues:

- Because of their proximity to the exterior and the fact that garage doors are often left open, garages tend to be a common location for termite—and other animal—infestations. You should do a thorough check of the garage, including moving any boxes or items blocking walls, to ensure that there is no major termite, rodent, or other animal damage, and that there are no current unwanted animal residents in the garage.

Life Expectancy

Garage doors will typically last 20 to 30 years.

Garage door openers will typically last ten to 20 years.

Scope of Work (SOW) Tasks

7

Garage doors and openers are pretty straightforward, and there are really only two tasks associated with this component:

REPLACE GARAGE DOOR	Garage doors will run anywhere from 7' wide to 15' wide (or perhaps bigger), depending on the size of the garage and the door configuration. A professional installer can replace just the door, replace the entire system (tracks and all), or install a new door system from scratch. The entire process will generally take two to four hours per door.
REPLACE DOOR OPENER	Garage door openers are fairly easy to install, especially if you're just doing a replacement. You can either have a professional garage door company do the installation or have your carpenter/handyman do it. If you have a garage door company do the work, they'll likely provide the materials, though if you have another contractor do the work, you can just pick up an opener from your local big-box store.

Cost Guidelines

The cost of garage door and opener installation are as follows:

REPLACE GARAGE DOOR	**$500-$1,200** The cost will mostly depend on the size of the door, with smaller, single doors costing in the $500-$600 range and larger, double doors costing in the $800-$1,200 range. Fancier doors or windows will add cost, and you can certainly spend upwards of $2,000 for custom doors if the resale of the house requires it.
REPLACE DOOR OPENER	**$200-$400** A typical garage door company will charge between $300 and $400 to replace a standard chain- or belt-driven opener, with chain-driven models being cheaper than their belt-driven counterparts. If you'd like to save some money, you can purchase a typical belt-driven or chain-driven model from a big box store for about $150-$200, and have your handyman install it for $50-$100. Keep in mind that larger doors (12' and above) will generally require higher horsepower motors for the opener and will have a higher materials cost.

7

Determining Your Local Prices

Most investors I know use local retail garage door companies for their garage door needs—just do an internet search. Garage doors are a competitive industry, so prices are generally consistent and reasonable among most companies. Most garage door companies are happy to give you prices for doors and openers over the phone. Make sure you have door measurements in hand, but don't expect much of a discount, even for repeat business—garage door services are a commodity and there isn't much of a margin for the contractor.

How to Pay for the Job

Most garage door work is done in less than one day, and it's typical for work to be paid for at completion.

COMPONENT #8
LANDSCAPING

Overview

Full landscaping jobs are beyond the scope of this text, but I do want to touch on some of the most common landscaping tasks and associated costs applicable when renovating a low- to mid-level house.

They include:

- Lawn maintenance
- Trim bushes
- Trim tree
- Remove tree
- Install sod
- Build retaining wall
- Heavy equipment work

Inspection Tips

When deciding whether to do landscaping at your property—and how much to do—consider the two reasons for doing any work:

1. Getting good listing photographs.
2. Making a good first impression on prospective buyers.

When you put the work in this context, it should help you identify the focus of your landscaping efforts.

The first thing I like to do is to determine what angles will be used to photograph the exterior of the property, and then have my designer or photographer make a recommendation on how landscaping efforts will improve the planned photography—for example, pruning back trees and bushes that obstruct the view of the property from the photographic angles or that will cause the photographs to be unbalanced or awkward.

Next, I will drive to the property, approaching from each street position that potential buyers will approach from, and see what aspects of the landscaping tend to stick out in a negative way. Perhaps there's a big bush that obstructs the view of the house from the street? Or maybe there's a big bare spot on the lawn directly next to the driveway. Are branches overhanging the house that might lead a buyer to be concerned about future roof damage or a squirrel invasion?

Too many investors will either spend *not enough* money on landscaping or they'll spend *too much* money. Remember, the goal of landscaping is good pictures and a good first impression; anything less than that is not enough, and anything more than that is probably wasted money.

Life Expectancy
N/A

Scope of Work (SOW) Tasks
Here are the most common landscaping tasks you'll likely undertake as a rehabber:

LAWN MAINTENANCE	To ensure the safety of my contractors, I will generally have my landscaper cut the lawn at the beginning of every job. Long grass can hide tools, nails, and other sharp objects, and when contractors are working around the exterior of the house, I want them to be safe.
	Additionally, many of the distressed houses I purchase have very little curb appeal when we buy them, so cutting the lawn and sprucing up the yard will quickly make the house look presentable again. This will make your neighbors happy (as well as the homeowners' association, if you have one), and will also draw the attention of passersby, which will be good for your resale prospects.
TRIM BUSHES	When I do my first lawn cutting, I'll also have the landscaper trim all the bushes. The most important trimming is of the bushes around the house. Bushes that touch the siding on the house make it very difficult for our exterior painters and siding installers to do their jobs, not to mention that bushes rubbing up against the siding will cause more wear and tear to the siding, shortening its lifespan.
	While the landscaper is trimming the bushes around the house, I'll have him trim the bushes on the rest of the property as well, again adding to the curb appeal and appeasing the neighbors who may have been staring at a dump for months or years before you bought the property.

TRIM TREES

There are three instances when I'll trim trees:
• When they overhang or touch the roof.
• When they obstruct the driveway or walkways.
• When they obstruct a clear view of the house.
   Any branches that are touching the roof are causing damage to the shingles; any branches that are overhanging the roof are dropping leaves and debris that fill gutters and decrease the lifespan of the shingles.
   Tree limbs that obstruct driveways or walkways are dangerous, and the last thing you want on your project is a lawsuit. I will cut all tree limbs to a minimum of 8' off the ground, so there is no danger of someone running into one, either with their car or body.
   When the view of a house is obstructed by a tree or tree limbs, it makes it very difficult to get a good exterior picture of the house, which is essential for your listing when you're trying to sell. Additionally, if you're going to spend lots of money making your house look good, you want people to be able to see it!

8

REMOVE TREE

If I have a dead or dying tree on my property, or if I have a tree that is situated in a precarious position—either risking falling on my house or a neighbor's house—I'll cut it down as soon as the project starts. I know of several investors who have had trees fall on their properties, and while insurance may cover the cost, the stress and added work is just not worth taking the risk.

INSTALL SOD

When it's necessary to tear up grass either for repairs, grading, or a redesign of a yard, it can take a long time for that grass to return. Selling a house with an ugly dirt yard can be difficult, and installing sod is a cost-effective alternative.
   If you'll be tearing up your yard during a renovation, I recommend doing the tearing up early in the project, as that will give your grass some time to grow back and you may be able to avoid the expense of laying sod.

BUILD RETAINING WALL	There are many different materials that can be used to build a retaining wall, including concrete blocks, wooden railroad ties, stone, or poured concrete. Each has its advantages and drawbacks. If you need a retaining wall on your property, it's likely that other houses in the neighborhood have them as well; look at the types of materials they use and try to use something with a similar look and feel to ensure that your house doesn't stick out in a negative way.
HEAVY EQUIPMENT WORK	Sometimes I'll need to bring in my landscaping company that does heavy equipment work. They can do tasks such as digging and excavation when I want to open up a piece of land, build retaining walls, or dig trenches for drainage.

Cost Guidelines

Here are some general cost guidelines for the landscaping tasks above:

LAWN MAINTENANCE	**$30-$60 per 1/4 acre** I will generally tell my landscaper to visit each of my properties every few weeks during the warmer months and cut the lawn when needed. I trust him to do the work when it needs to be done and not do work if it doesn't need to be done. For the repeat business on multiple houses, he will generally provide a reasonable price and great service. There are many factors that will influence the cost of a particular job, including the terrain, steep grades or slopes, or excessively tall grass, but I've found that this price range is pretty consistent across many properties.
TRIM BUSHES	**$30-$60** This is the cost to trim all the bushes for a typical yard that is a bit overgrown and in need of sprucing up. This includes cutting all bushes away from the house so that they're not touching the siding, trimming other bushes around the property, and trimming the low-hanging branches on trees around the property.

TRIM TREE	**$100-$250 per 30'-60' tree** The actual cost will depend on the location of the tree, the height of the tree, what is under the tree, and whether any special equipment is needed.
REMOVE TREE	**$100-$1,500** The actual cost will depend on the location of the tree, the height of the tree, the type of tree and the clearance around the tree. For a 30' tree not obstructed by power lines or a house, expect to pay $250-$350. Also, expect to pay extra if you want the stump ground or removed. This will typically run $50-$75.
INSTALL SOD	**$1-$2 per square foot** If you plan to do the installation yourself, expect to pay $.30-$.50 per square foot for the materials alone. Larger areas will tend to be lower in price, while smaller installations will have a higher per square foot cost.
BUILD RETAINING WALL	**Concrete block: $30-$50 per square foot of wall.** **Wood: $20-$40 per square foot of wall.** **Stone: $30-$50 per square foot of wall.** **Poured concrete: $30-$50 per square foot of wall.** While you can have a landscaping company build your retaining walls, they will likely charge a good bit more than a company specializing in heavy equipment (though they may be one and the same). If you need intricate detail in your wall, or if there is a complex installation, your prices can quickly escalate. Also keep in mind that while many taller retaining walls (over 6') have historically been built with wood or wood railroad ties, local codes in most places today will require these taller walls to be built with block or concrete. Always check your local building codes before building any structural walls, including retaining walls.

HEAVY EQUIPMENT WORK	**$1,000-$2,000 per day** Many heavy equipment companies are willing to provide most of their basic equipment plus two or three workers on a daily basis for somewhere in this price range.

Determining Your Local Prices

You'll likely use three different contractors for your landscaping needs:

- Small lawn maintenance company for cutting and trimming bushes.
- Tree service for trimming and removing trees.
- Heavy equipment company for work such as grading or excavating.

While you can call around and ask for general prices (and you'll probably get them), heavy landscaping work is always going to be a custom job, and the actual prices will vary depending on the specific work needing to be done. Also remember that weather conditions and time of year may have a significant effect on any exterior renovation costs.

8

How to Pay for the Job

For small jobs, I'll generally pay when the work is completed. For larger jobs, I'll generally pay part upfront (especially when materials are needed) and the rest when the work is complete.

COMPONENT #9
SEPTIC SYSTEM

Overview

In houses that don't have public sewage hook-ups, such as houses in rural areas or older neighborhoods, waste disposal is handled by a septic system. A septic system takes water and waste from the house, filters out the liquid waste, and stores the solid waste for future removal.

A septic system consists of two main components:
1. Septic tank
2. Leaching field

SEPTIC TANK

The septic tank is a large concrete box buried several feet below ground on the side or in the back of the house. The septic tank is the first place the sewage travels when it leaves the house. The septic tank holds the solid waste and releases the liquid waste; in addition, over time, some of the solid waste will decompose into liquid waste and be expelled from the tank.

When the liquid—known as "effluent"—is expelled from the tank, it travels through a pipe to the leaching field.

LEACHING FIELD

The effluent travels to the leaching field—also known as leaching bed, disposal field, or drain field—and is deposited into the soil through a network of perforated pipes.

The septic system should be inspected by a qualified septic company prior to purchasing the property, as major repairs to the septic system can be extremely costly and can easily change the value of a deal if you have to pay for the repairs. Septic systems will generally need to be cleaned and emptied every three to five years, and you should budget for this cleaning regardless of when the last cleaning took place, as most buyers will require evidence that the system has been inspected, serviced, and cleaned prior to sale.

Inspection Tips

Any time you're considering purchasing a house on septic, I highly recommend that you bring in a septic company to inspect the system and clean the tank. Determining the condition of the system without the appropriate knowledge and tools is nearly impossible, and the cost of having to repair or replace a system is too great to leave to chance.

That said, there are a few things to check and a few signs to be aware of when doing a cursory inspection of a house with a septic system:

- When a septic system fails, the leaching field will often lose its ability to absorb effluent. If you know where it is, do a walk of the leaching field and look for any damp spots or standing fluid. If you can't attribute these wet areas to rain or other recent weather activities, there's a reasonable chance that the leaching field has failed.
- Note any objectionable smells, both around the leaching field and in the bathrooms of the property.
- If the toilets or sinks are backed up and not flowing properly, this could be an indication of a failed or full septic tank.

Life Expectancy

Septic tank: Indefinitely, if properly maintained and cleaned.

Leaching field: 30 to 40 years, after which a new field will need to be built.

9

Scope of Work (SOW) Tasks

The following are the typical SOW tasks associated with septic systems:

INSPECT AND CLEAN SEPTIC TANK	You must have a septic inspection *prior* to purchasing the property, and during this inspection, you may want to schedule a cleaning of the tank. While it may cost more to have the contractor return after you purchase the property to do the cleaning, you shouldn't wait to have the inspection, as any major repairs could be very costly, and you don't want to learn of these problems only after the house is purchased. If the house has a septic system, you should always factor in this cost.

MAJOR SEPTIC REPAIRS	Major septic repairs include building a new leaching field, repairing the septic tank, or repairing damaged sewage pipes coming from the house to the septic system. These repairs can be very costly (sometimes upwards of $10,000) and should be investigated *prior* to purchase.

Cost Guidelines

Here is what you can expect to pay for septic related tasks:

INSPECT AND CLEAN SEPTIC TANK	**$300-$500** This will generally include the labor involved in finding the buried septic tank, digging to the top opening, inspecting the system, cleaning the system, and providing a diagnosis of any issues relating to the system.
MAJOR SEPTIC REPAIRS	**$1,000-$10,000+** Major septic repairs can run into the tens of thousands of dollars. If you have an inspection done that indicates major septic issues, it's probably worth getting a second opinion, and it may be worth re-negotiating or backing out of your contract for the property.

Determining Your Local Prices

A quick phone call to a few septic companies found online should give you an idea of what the standard inspection and cleaning costs are in your area.

How to Pay for the Job

Typically, the cost of an inspection or cleaning will be paid upon completion of the work, which should take only a few hours, barring any issues.

COMPONENT #10
FOUNDATION

Overview

It would take an entire book to cover the range of foundation work you might see on a typical house—in fact, engineers spend years in school learning about these issues.

When it comes to foundation concerns, I highly recommend consulting with a qualified professional. In fact, I highly recommend working with both a structural engineer, who can determine the scope of the problem and the required fix, and a qualified contractor, who can tell you how much it will cost to do the work. When I assess foundation or structural issues, I will get my engineer and my carpenter together at the house to review the problem and the fix together, to ensure they are on the same page. This allows me to avoid having to translate between the two of them, which I would have to do if I met with them separately.

Also, any time you get a recommendation from a structural engineer that you plan to implement, make sure you get the recommendation in writing and with the engineer's stamp. Not only will this be useful when a building inspector wants to review your plans, but if there is ever an issue with the fix, the engineer will take some or all of the liability, instead of you or your contractors.

Additionally, after a contractor completes work recommended by a structural engineer, I highly recommend paying the engineer to come back, review the work, and sign off on the fact that it was completed to his specifications. This too will reduce any liability you might have should the fix not be sufficient to solve the problem.

Inspection Tips

Here are some tips for determining if you might have a foundation problem with your property:

- Floors that are not level.
- Doors that don't close properly (out of plumb).
- Cracks in walls, especially over doorways and windows.
- Large cracks in concrete floors.
- Basement walls that are bowing or have horizontal cracks.

While not all of these issues will always indicate a foundation problem, if you see one or more of them, it's worth consulting with an expert before proceeding with a house purchase, as foundation problems can be costly to repair.

One foundation issue I want to address in more detail—because it is likely the most common issue you'll run into—is a bowing foundation wall in a basement. In many older homes and in many parts of the country, it is not uncommon to see basement walls that are bowing horizontally or even have horizontal cracks through the wall. Often, a horizontal crack is the result of static pressure from the soil on the other side of the wall. The grading or run-off is bad, water seeps into the soil and puts pressure on the wall, and eventually it gives and cracks. If you don't do anything, the wall will eventually cave in.

Depending on the severity of the problem (the amount of bowing), the solution could involve using Kevlar strips or steel plates to anchor the wall in place. If the wall is near collapse, or if the wall is more than 1/2" out of plumb, it may be necessary to excavate along the exterior of the wall, straighten it, and then support the wall using steel beams.

Life Expectancy

The foundation should last the lifetime of the structure.

10

Scope of Work (SOW) Tasks

Here are a couple of tasks to consider when looking at a property with potential foundation issues:

ENGINEER CONSULTATION	Most engineers will charge an hourly rate to visit a property, diagnose a problem, recommend a solution, and provide a written report. For a typical foundation issue, expect three to six hours of an engineer's time. This includes a final inspection and sign-off of the work done by your contractors.

FIXING BOWED OR CRACKED FOUNDATION WALL	For a bowed or cracked basement wall, you'll want one or more qualified foundation repair companies to make recommendations on how to fix the problem and to provide estimates of the work. You should ensure that the company pulls the proper permits for the repairs and that they provide a warranty for the work. I like to get a lifetime warranty, as it makes any future buyers more comfortable with the repair.
OTHER FOUNDATION REPAIR	For any foundation-related concerns, you'll want to consult with a qualified engineer and have a qualified contractor perform the work the engineer recommends. Ensure that the work is done to the engineer's specifications, pull any required permits, and when possible get a warranty on the work.

Cost Guidelines

Here are some basic cost guidelines for foundation work:

ENGINEER CONSULTATION	**$75-$150 per hour**
FIXING BOWED OR CRACKED FOUNDATION WALL	**$100-$300 per linear foot** This is a very general estimate at what it might cost to fix a bowing foundation wall. The actual price could be a lot less if an engineer determines that the shifting is no longer an issue or could be a lot more if the issue is severe or if there are other circumstances that are contributing to the problem.
OTHER FOUNDATION REPAIR	**$500-$10,000+** Foundation repairs can be as little as a few hundred dollars up to tens of thousands of dollars. In some cases, you may run into a problem that is impossible to fix without tearing down the house and starting over. It's very difficult to generalize the cost of foundation repairs, so make sure to work with a qualified engineer and contractor.

10

Determining Your Local Prices

Every foundation issue is going to be unique, and every foundation repair company's price will be based on the scope of the specific job. Unfortunately, there is no good way to generalize foundation prices or to determine if a company is competitively priced without comparing bids for the same job. If you run into a foundation issue, get a recommendation from a qualified engineer, and then get multiple bids from qualified contractors to complete the work.

How to Pay for the Job

Most reputable foundation repair companies will want most or all of the payment at the completion of the work. In some cases, they will want a down payment, which should be paid just prior to start of work. If you'll be working with independent contractors (a carpenter, for example) instead of a foundation repair company, it will be up to you and the contractor to negotiate a payment schedule based on the scope of the work, the length of the job, and the amount of materials required.

10

COMPONENT #11
DEMO

Overview

As a rehabber, there are two components of demo that you need to be aware of:

1. Providing a dumpster for the debris.
2. The labor involved in the demo work.

In any large town or city, there are going to be several companies that provide roll-off dumpsters (big dumpsters that "roll off" the truck and onto the driveway and then can be rolled back onto the truck and removed when they're full). Even in smaller towns, there are typically at least one or two companies that provide this service.

They will generally have various sized dumpsters, from 10 cubic yards (approximately 12' × 8' × 4') through 40 cubic yards (approximately 22' × 8' × 8') and several sizes in between. The 30 cubic yard dumpster is the most common and is typically big enough for a cosmetic demo of a standard 3-bedroom house. You can generally call to order the dumpster the same day or the day before you need it delivered, but don't procrastinate—make sure the dumpster is onsite prior to demo starting. If a contractor has to demo one day and then move all the debris to a dumpster another day, he won't be happy with the extra time and work, and his prices will reflect that.

While there are specialists out there who do nothing but demo, I will generally use one of my other contractors (handyman or carpenter) to do demo at the beginning of a project. Demo isn't very complex, but you'll want someone who has some experience in doing it, as poor demo work can result in having to spend more on the rehab to fix the issues the uncontrolled demo caused. There is an easy way and a hard way when it comes to removing things like appliances, light fixtures, plumbing fixtures, cabinets, and flooring. Contractors who know how to do it the easy way will save you time, money, and stress.

Inspection Tips

N/A

Life Expectancy
N/A

Scope of Work (SOW) Tasks
Here are the two tasks associated with most demo tasks:

ROLL-OFF DUMPSTER	Dumpsters range in size from 10 through 40 cubic yards. Call at least a day in advance to ensure there is enough time to deliver prior to demo starting. Most dumpster companies will allow you to keep the dumpster for at least ten days, and you can usually negotiate a longer time frame if necessary, especially if you provide repeat business. One word of warning—if you leave an empty dumpster in front of your house, there is a good chance your neighbors (or people just driving by) will fill it for you. I've probably had more trash thrown in my dumpsters by other people than from my own debris. It's infuriating that people would just fill up a dumpster without asking you first, but it happens, and you should be prepared. Have the dumpster delivered right before demo starts and try to get as much as you can into it on day one before others start to throw their crap in there.
DEMO LABOR	To get maximum use out of the dumpster, your contractors should batch all the demo work at the same time. Demo is messy and getting it out of the way all at once will make the rest of the project go more smoothly.
PORTA POTTY	If you'll be running a jobsite with no running water or working toilets, it's a good idea to have a Porta Potty on site for your contractors. This will keep them from having to leave the job throughout the day and will also keep them from getting "creative" with how they relieve themselves.

11

Cost Guidelines

Here is what you should expect to pay for demo-related tasks:

ROLL-OFF DUMPSTER	**$350-$600, depending on dumpster size.**
	Dumpster costs are pretty standardized within an area, and the biggest contributing factor to the price will be the size of the dumpster you choose. In general, go a little bit bigger than you need, as you'll have more debris than you expect. Don't forget about things like boxes from your fixtures and appliances, carpet debris from you carpet installation, etc. when determining your dumpster size.
	When ordering a roll-off dumpster, expect that you will have a specific time period in which to use the dumpster (about two weeks) and also a maximum weight allowance for the debris you fill it with (generally, 2-4 tons, depending on the size of the dumpster).
	Finally, note that if you order the dumpster too far in advance of needing it, you'll find that neighbors will start to fill it for you. For this reason, we highly recommend not having your dumpster delivered until the last possible minute and filling it as quickly as possible once it arrives.
DEMO LABOR	**$10-$15 per hour per laborer; or** **$.50-$1.00 per square foot for full cosmetic demo of a house.**
	While you could probably determine individual demo prices for different parts of the job (cabinets versus flooring, for example), most contractors will estimate their demo prices based on how long it will take them to do the work. I like to pay my demo workers anywhere from $10-$15/hour, depending on the complexity of the job (things like lots of stairs, small spaces, or heavy debris demand more money), and some more experienced demo workers will base their price on the size of the house when doing a full cosmetic gut of the house.

11

PORTA POTTY	**$100-$200 per month**
	The supplier will drop the Porta Potty off at your site, stop by about once a week to clean it, and then pick it up at the completion of the job.
	Many companies will charge more for the first month, and then provide a discount for additional months, so the longer you rent the potty, the less it costs on a weekly or monthly basis.

Determining Your Local Prices

If your demo workers are working on an hourly rate, you can just ask how much they charge per hour. But many demo workers will want to bid the whole job and will need to see the job before they give a bid. There's no easy way to describe the scope of a demo job over the phone, so it's not easy to get bids without the contractors actually seeing the job.

How to Pay for the Job

The dumpster company will likely charge you at the time of delivery. The crew doing the demo shouldn't be paid until the work is completed, as they shouldn't have any material costs or overhead.

11

COMPONENT #12
PLUMBING

Overview

I like to think of the plumbing system in a house as containing five main components:

1. Water source: well or municipal
2. Water heater
3. Distribution piping
4. Drain piping/venting
5. Fixtures

WATER SOURCE: WELL OR MUNICIPAL

Water is supplied to the house in one of two ways: either from a well located on the property or from the local municipality via pipes in the street.

For houses that rely on wells for their water, there are two types of wells—shallow (less than 50 feet deep) and deep (more than 50 feet and up to several hundred feet deep). Wells rely on pumps to move the water from the well to the house, and these pumps can be located in the well (common for deep wells) or exterior to the well, perhaps even in the basement of the house (common for shallow wells).

In conjunction with the pump is a water pressure tank that usually resides in the basement, where the water line comes into the house. This tank is used to store water and to provide water pressure to the house.

Houses that rely on water from the city will have a main line coming into the house from the street. This line will generally run underground from the street in front of the house to the interior of the house, in the shortest configuration possible. In other words, if you're trying to determine where the main water line comes into the house, start at the front of the garage or along the basement wall closest to the street. There will be a water meter—used to measure the amount of water coming into the house to generate your water bill—either near the street or in the basement of the house where the main line comes in. Also, there should be a main water shutoff valve where the main line comes in. When this shutoff valve is closed, no water will run through the house. It's important to know where this is, in case there is ever a major leak in the house and you need to completely shut off the water.

The other major component you should be aware of at this point in the plumbing system is the pressure reducing valve (PRV). This mechanical device is used to regulate the pressure in the house, reducing the high pressure of the incoming water to a more comfortable pressure for the fixtures in the house.

Typically, the PRV will keep the water pressure between 30-60 pounds per square inch (psi). If the PRV fails, water pressure will increase above this acceptable threshold and you may hear rattling in your pipes or have issues with your plumbing fixtures. When this happens, your PRV will need to be replaced. Depending on the water pressure from the municipal water supply and how well it is maintained, a PRV may last as short as ten years or as long as the life of the house.

WATER HEATER

If you follow the water line past the main shutoff valve, the first major appliance you will see is the water heater. Water comes directly into the house and into the water heater, where water is heated to supply hot water to the house.

The water heater may run on gas or electricity, with gas being more common these days. Gas water heaters use gas to light a pilot that starts a flame, which heats the water in the tank; electric water heaters contain a heating element that heats water much like an electric stove heats water in a pot.

Water heaters generally hold 30 to 50 gallons of water and last eight to ten years. From the water heater, there will be two lines—one for hot water and one for cold water. These two lines will branch off and supply water to all the fixtures throughout the house.

DISTRIBUTION PIPING

The distribution piping consists of all the hot and cold-water lines branching through the house. In most cases, the hot and cold lines will run next to each other to each of the fixtures.

These supply lines are generally made of copper, steel, or a plastic material (PVC or CPVC), though Pex (a flexible plastic piping material) is exceptionally cheap, easy to use, and is becoming more common these days.

Copper, PVC, and Pex piping should last for the life of the house, and unless there is specific damage to the piping, you shouldn't have to worry about rust or deterioration.

DRAIN PIPING/VENTING

All sinks, tubs, and toilets will have larger pipes—generally 3"-4" in diameter—that take waste and water from the fixture to a main drain line (called the "stack") that runs vertically from below the foundation of the house (where the wastewater is taken from the house) all the way up through the roof, where it ends with a vent open to the air.

The top of the stack is vented out through the roof in order to maintain neutral air pressure in the system and to allow sewage gases to escape so that the gas doesn't end up back in the house, causing sickness and odor. The drain line from each fixture will tie into the main stack at two points: towards the bottom of the stack where the wastewater flows and towards the top of the stack to allow the gas to escape.

At its lowest point in the house, the stack turns and runs horizontally, draining out of the house to link up with the city sewer or the septic system.

Drain lines are commonly made of PVC, especially in houses built after the 1960s. In older houses, it is not uncommon to see drain lines made of galvanized steel, cast iron, copper, or even lead. For the most part, drain lines of all material will often last the life of the house.

FIXTURES

The plumbing fixtures include all the things the supply and drain lines hook up to, including sinks and faucets, tubs and showers, toilets, dishwasher, washing machine, and hose bibs (exterior connectors where hoses attach).

12

Inspection Tips

When inspecting the plumbing of a home you're considering purchasing, the primary goal is to rule out any costly repairs. In many cases, you'll be replacing cosmetic plumbing fixtures like toilets, faucets, and sinks, so any minor issues related to those are likely to be repaired during a basic renovation.

While it's unlikely you'll be familiar with all plumbing codes in your area—I've been doing this a long time and I'm not familiar with all my local codes—there are still many basic plumbing items you can identify during your inspection. Remember, even identifying potential issues will allow you to bring in an expert to examine more closely and help you avoid any expensive surprises down the road.

- If the property's water source is a well, there are a couple of things you will want to verify, and would be wise to bring in an expert to assist:

  First, if the property relies on well water, you should include a contingency in your contract that will allow you to get the water tested. Contaminated wells can be one of the costliest issues you ever face, as there may not be any cost-effective fix.

  Next, if the property was previously on a well, and either a new well has been dug or the property is now on municipal water, you should bring in an expert to verify that the old well was properly abandoned. This is now a requirement in many jurisdictions, and the cost of properly abandoning a well can run well into the thousands of dollars for deep wells.

- If your property is served by city water, there are two tests I like to perform that will give an indication of any plumbing leaks on the property:

  First, to test if there are any interior water leaks, turn off all the water sources in the property and then find the water meter. On many water meters, there is an indication of whether water is flowing or not—for example, a spinning mechanical arrow. If the water meter indicates that water is flowing through it—but all the interior plumbing fixtures are off—this can be an indication of a leak somewhere past the meter.

  Second, if your water meter sits at the street near your property line, you can turn the interior water off at the main water shutoff valve and observe the meter. If water is flowing through the meter when the main shutoff is closed, this is an indication of a leak between the meter and the shutoff valve. In many cases, that leak will be in the main line running from the street to the house.

- The next thing I will do when inspecting the plumbing system at a potential property is to determine whether the water heater should be replaced. There are several things you should look for and consider:

  First, try to determine the age of the heater. Typically, there is a sticker or plaque attached to the side or top of the heater that contains basic information—manufacturer, model number, serial number, etc. In many cases, the manufacturer date will be listed here as well. In some cases, you can glean the manufacturer year from the serial number. If the water heater is more than eight years old, you should seriously consider replacing it.

A common failure point of water heaters is that the bottom will rust, and water will leak out of the tank. Obviously, large amounts of water leaking from the tank can do major damage to the house, so I recommend taking a thorough look around and under the water heater to rule out any major rust or leaks. If you see rust on or under the heater, I recommend replacing it to reduce your risk of a major leak.

You will want to verify that the size of the water heater is appropriate for the size of the house and the number of bathrooms. If the property has more than one bathroom and you expect more than two people will be living in the property, you should ensure that the water heater is a minimum of 40 to 50 gallons. For three-bathroom properties and above, consider a larger tank of 60 to 80 gallons.

You should check to see if the water heater has an expansion tank attached. Its purpose is to prevent the pressure from the heated water from being too high. If there isn't one, depending on the scope of your repairs and whether you need to pull permits, you might want to consider adding one. This may be required to bring the water heater up to code.

Finally, you should turn on the hot water at one or more fixtures to verify that the water heater is working properly and heating the water. If the water doesn't get hot, on a gas water heater, you can check the pilot light to ensure its lit. On an electric water heater, the heating element will sometimes burn out before the water heater has reached the end of its life—if this happens, the element can be replaced without having to replace the entire heater.

12

Next, I recommend looking at the supply lines running from the water heater to the rest of the house. Not only should you be looking at the condition of these lines but also considering the material they are made of. Here are a few things to look for:

- If you have a house that is more than 80 years old, you should determine if the supply lines are made of cast iron, steel, or lead piping. For cast iron and steel piping, a thorough inspection of condition is recommended; for lead piping, I recommend getting the water tested to ensure that lead isn't contaminating the water.
- If you have a house that is more than 50 years old, you should verify that it doesn't have galvanized steel piping; if it does, the piping is likely

reaching the end of its life (it rusts from the inside out) and should be replaced. You can typically identify galvanized pipe by its gray color, threaded joints, and metallic tone when tapped with a screwdriver.

- In houses built in the 1980s and early 1990s, a material called polybutylene was commonly used for supply lines. This is typically a flexible gray plastic pipe and often has the letters "PB" stamped on it. It was later realized that this material breaks down over ten to 20 years and will eventually fail. If you have polybutylene plumbing in your house, you should seriously consider getting all the supply lines replaced prior to reselling; in many cases, this will be a red flag to both inspectors and lenders.

- I recommend testing every plumbing fixture in the house. This includes faucets, showers, toilets, appliances, and hose bibs. Even if you plan to replace some or all of these fixtures, testing them can reveal leaks, backups, and water pressure issues that you otherwise might not catch until after you've finalized your budget.

- If you have any concerns about the proper functioning of the drain lines or sewer line, you can close and fill all the sinks and tubs, and then allow them all to drain at the same—flushing the toilets simultaneously. If any of the fixtures drain slowly, or not at all, this can be an indication of clog or backup.

- Lastly, you should check for water stains under sinks and discoloration on ceilings, which can be indications of water leaks.

Life Expectancy

12

Life expectancy of the major plumbing components is covered in the section above.

Scope of Work (SOW) Tasks

Plumbing is one of the largest and most complex systems in the house, and therefore the range of possible renovation tasks is quite large. Below, I will detail the most common repairs you'll experience and the specific circumstances under which you'll want to complete them:

SERVICE CALL	Any time a plumber visits your property, he will charge a minimum fee for his time and expertise. This minimum is generally referred to as a "service fee" or "service call fee."
REPLACE MAIN LINE	If you turn off the water to your house at the first main shutoff valve past the plumbing meter (on the house side of the meter), you should be able to observe the meter to determine if any water is flowing through it. If the house water supply is turned off, but water is still flowing through the meter, the likely culprit is a leak in the main line. Another indication of a burst main line is if you notice water percolating to the top of the soil or wet soil between the street and the house where the plumbing line is likely to be coming in. If you notice either of these things, you should have a plumber investigate as soon as possible, as a burst main line can cause serious issues, including soil erosion around the foundation.
REPLACE PRV	If you notice that the water pressure in the house seems higher than what is typical, or if you hear rattling in the pipes when water is turned on, it's possible that the pressure reducing valve (PRV) has failed and the water pressure in the house is much too high. High water pressure is uncomfortable for the occupants and can also cause damage to plumbing fixtures and appliances. If you notice these things, you should have a plumber investigate. It's quick and easy for a plumber to test the water pressure in the house to determine if the PRV needs to be replaced.

12

REPLACE WATER HEATER

If the water heater in your house is more than eight years old (and certainly if it's more than ten years old), if you notice that the bottom of the heater is rusty or leaking, or if the heater is not heating water (no flame on a gas heater or heating element not working on an electric heater), it's probably time to replace the water heater.

In many jurisdictions, building codes will require an additional tank (called an expansion tank) to be attached to the heater to handle any water overflow from the heater due to increased pressure from the heated water. If your plumber installs this tank (and charges you for it), it's likely your local building codes require it.

In general, I like to replace the water heater if there is any possibility that it is near the end of its life. Not only can a failed heater cause a mess if it leaks, but many inspectors will note if a water heater is old and your buyer will request you to replace it prior to the sale closing. It's easier to just do it while the rest of the rehab is underway.

REPLACE ALL SUPPLY LINES

In some cases, you may need to replace all the supply lines in your house. This is most common when you have a bad piping material (such as polybutylene), when your plumbing has been stolen (copper pipes are often the target of thieves), or when you have an exceptionally old house with rusted galvanized steel or dangerous lead piping.

Repiping a house may be very easy if there is a basement with ceiling access, an open attic or crawl-space, or no sheetrock in the house; or it may be very difficult if existing plumbing runs under a slab or if pipes run in hard to reach areas or behind sheet-rocked walls. More complex repiping jobs will take longer and will be costlier, but a typical 3-bedroom, 2-bathroom house can generally be fully repiped in a day or less.

12

REPLACE TUB/ SHOWER COMBO UNITS

Many houses these days use pre-formed fiberglass tubs, showers or tub/shower combos that can be purchased off the shelf from big-box stores. This is the alternative to a stand-alone steel tub or a custom-built tile shower.

I will normally use these fiberglass tub/shower combos in my houses, unless I am doing something relatively high-end, in which case I'll build a tile shower in the master bath and still use the fiberglass tub/ showers in the secondary bathrooms.

Installing a new fiberglass tub—especially in an area where one didn't exist before—may require some additional framing work, so make sure you discuss tub installation with your carpenter during the framing stage of the renovation and before the tub is to be installed.

BUILD TILE SHOWER

In higher-end remodels, tiled showers are standard. These custom showers can be built to any size or shape specification, and the use of custom tile designs can make your shower distinctive. These custom showers will either have an off-the-shelf plastic base that is installed before the rest of the shower is built and tiled or will have a poured concrete base that allows the base of the shower to be tiled as well. Custom showers will generally require some custom framing and extra sheetrock work, so be sure to discuss the shower design with your carpenter and sheetrocker before having your plumber or tile installer start work. Also, because the tile work for a custom shower is often intricate, I would recommend not skimping on price when it comes to your tile installer—good tile work will stand out in a good way, while bad tile work will stand out in a very bad way.

Lastly, note that most custom showers will require custom glass or glass door solutions.

The specific set of tasks associated with installing a custom shower are:
- Framing (to be part of the framing component)
- Sheetrock/cement-board (to be part of the sheetrock component)
- Installing off-the-shelf base or pouring concrete base and attaching to drain.
- Tiling and grouting
- Installing glass and door

12

INSTALL OR REPLACE SINKS

If you'll be replacing kitchen or vanity bathroom sinks, you'll need to budget for the labor and materials cost of sink replacement. Even if you'll be keeping the sinks, if you plan to replace kitchen cabinets or bathroom vanities, you'll need to pay the labor cost of sink replacement, as the plumber will need to pull the sink out of the old cabinet and install it in the new cabinet.

I usually always replace sinks when I replace cabinets or vanities and will often replace drop-in steel kitchen sinks even if I don't replace the kitchen cabinets, as these steel sinks tend to get rusty and stained. If you plan to get new bathroom vanities, make sure you note the size and shape of the hole that is drilled into the vanity for the sinks so that you can buy the correct replacement sinks.

INSTALL OR REPLACE FAUCETS

If you'll be replacing kitchen or bathroom faucets, you'll need to budget for the labor and materials cost of faucet replacement. Even if you'll be keeping the faucets, if you plan to replace kitchen cabinets or bathroom vanities, you'll need to pay the labor cost of faucet replacement, as the plumber will need to pull the faucet out of the old cabinet or sink and install it in the new cabinet or sink.

I always replace all the faucets in the house, unless the existing faucets are brand new and match the look and feel of the other fixtures I use throughout the house.

INSTALL OR REPLACE SHOWER/TUB HARDWARE

I always replace all tub and shower hardware when doing a renovation.

If the existing hardware is relatively new (less than 15 years old) and a standard model, you can generally just replace the trim kit (the parts of the hardware that can be seen, such as the knobs and the stem/showerhead). But if you're installing a new tub/shower combo, if the existing hardware is very old or if the existing model is not standard, you'll need to replace both the trim kit and the internal mechanism of the hardware as well (called the "mixer").

Make sure you know if you need just the trim kit or the entire mechanism, so that you can buy the appropriate materials.

12

INSTALL OR REPLACE TOILET	I always replace all toilets when doing a renovation. Personally, I hate the thought of using someone else's toilet when I move into a house, and buyers appreciate clean and new toilets in their new house.
REPLACE WASHER BOX	The washer box is the plastic box that holds the hot and cold water hookups and the drain hole for the laundry washing machine. If these lines and drain don't exist, or if any of the lines are leaking, it is generally easier to install a whole new washer box than to try to fix the existing components.
	If you see mold around the sheetrock or baseboards in the laundry area, it's likely due to leaks in the lines coming in and out of the washer box and is a good indication the washer box should be replaced. Note that replacing the washer box—and fixing the lines coming in and out of it—may require some sheetrock patching, depending on the exact location of the leak and the existing sheetrock damage.
INSTALL OR REPLACE DISHWASHER	Most dishwashers will use a supply line branched off from the kitchen sink and a drain line that attaches to the drain at the kitchen sink. These lines are often run behind or through the base cabinets between the sink and the dishwasher and then are hooked up to the dishwasher.
	If these lines already exist (for example, if you're replacing an existing dishwasher in the same location), the plumber will just need to hook up the existing lines to the new dishwasher. If they don't exist, he'll need to run the lines as well as hook them up both at the dishwasher and at the sink.

12

FIX LEAKS

Plumbing leaks come in all shapes and sizes. In some cases, the leaky pipe is easily accessed and repaired (for example, under a sink) and in some cases the leaky pipe is tremendously difficult to access and repair (for example, when the leak is under a concrete foundation slab).

Under-slab leaks are generally the most complicated and costly to fix; the process involves locating the leak, jack-hammering the concrete, fixing the pipe, and then patching the concrete. In some cases, it's easier for the plumber to bypass the leak by abandoning the pipes under the slab and running new pipes through the house—above the slab—therefore not requiring any concrete demo or repair.

A good plumber will always evaluate solutions that don't require concrete work or demolition of other expensive parts of the house.

In many cases, expect to pay an hourly rate for leak fixes. Because it can often be difficult to pinpoint the problem and implement a solution, plumbers prefer to work on an hourly basis rather than give a fixed quote prior to solving the problem.

UNCLOG DRAINS

If you have drains in your house that don't flow well, it may be the result of a localized clog in a drain line other than the main drain line, or it may be a result of a clog in the main drain. If multiple drains are backing up, that's an indication of a main drain line clog.

Plumbers have several solutions for resolving clogged drains, depending on the location, source, and severity of the clog.

Generally, expect to pay an hourly rate for fixing clogged drain lines.

12

Cost Guidelines

Here is what to expect in terms of plumbing costs:

SERVICE CALL	**$60-$100** If you have a plumber visit your property for any reason, expect to pay for a service call, which typically amounts to the cost of an hour of the plumber's time. So, even if the work you need done only requires ten minutes of work and no materials, you should still expect to pay this minimum fee.
REPLACE MAIN LINE	**$1,500-$3,000 for standard replacement** **$3,000+ in areas where building codes are more stringent, or when repairing or replacing a line under a slab.** The price range will likely be determined by which part of the country you live in. In exceptionally cold climates, codes will require that main lines be made of galvanized steel or copper, and be buried very deep, below the frost line (4' or more). This increases the cost tremendously in those areas. Also, this price assumes that the length is less than 100' run of pipe from street to house and that there are no major obstacles in the way of replacing the pipe. In many cases, the plumber can avoid digging a trench to replace the pipe by attaching the new pipe to one end of the old pipe and literally pulling the new pipe through the existing trench while removing the old pipe at the same time. This can help avoid having to tear up driveways and other concrete paths that the pipe might run under. Also note that in some cases, the main line will run some distance under the slab of a house before it connects to the water heater; if the main line breaks under the slab of the house, it's likely your plumber will need to cut through the concrete slab to repair the line, potentially adding thousands of dollars to the cost of repairs.
REPLACE PRV	**$150-$300** The cost of the valve itself will be $40-$100, depending on the type and quality, and the work should take a qualified plumber about an hour.

12

REPLACE WATER HEATER

$550-$1,050

If you plan to purchase the materials yourself at a big box store, expect the costs to break down as follows:

Labor: $150-$250

Materials: $400-$800

This cost should include the removal of the old water heater, replacement with a standard 30-50-gallon tank, and then disposal of the old parts. The work should take a qualified plumber a couple hours.

There tends to be about $200 price difference between 30-gallon and 40-gallon water heaters and between 40-gallon and 50-gallon water heaters, but I highly recommend paying for a larger tank in any house that has at least two bathrooms. This will be a selling feature and your buyers will appreciate it.

REPLACE ALL SUPPLY LINES

$250-$350 per fixture

The cost to repipe a house with all new supply lines is generally based on the number of fixtures that are being replumbed. Fixtures include toilets, faucets, shower/tub hook-ups, dishwasher, washing machine lines, and hose bibs.

A standard 3-bedroom, 2-bathroom house will have 15 to 20 fixtures, and repiping should cost somewhere around $4,000-$7,000. The work should take one or two qualified plumbers a full day. This price does not include any drywall repairs that will need to be made after repiping is completed.

INSTALL OR REPLACE SHOWER/TUB

Labor: $250-$500

Materials: $300-$600

This assumes a standard 3-piece fiberglass tub surround that you can purchase at any of the big-box stores.

Keep in mind that the labor price could be higher if there is extra work to level the floor, replace any studs that the tub needs to be attached to, or replace insulation behind the tub.

12

BUILD TILE SHOWER

Labor: $20-$30 per square foot of tiled space

Materials: $3-$10 per square foot of tiled space

This labor price will include both the plumber and the tile installation cost, plus the cost of installing either a pre-fabricated plastic shower base or a cement base that will be tiled over. The material price will include the tile, the grout, the cement, and the installation materials.

Before the shower is tiled, the walls will need to be built to specification. This work should be covered under the framing component. Once the walls are built, your plumber will be responsible for installing a pre-form plastic shower base or pouring a concrete base that can be tiled over. Your tile guy will likely be responsible for installing the cement board, tiling the walls and floor, and grouting the tile. Expect this work to take up to a week.

INSTALL OR REPLACE SINKS

Labor: $50-$100

Materials: $30-$150

A typical bathroom vanity sink will cost $30-$60 and a typical stainless-steel drop-in kitchen sink will cost $100-$150 for low- to mid-level quality. The price includes both installation of the sink and reconnecting the drain line.

If you'll be installing granite countertops, the cost to provide and install sinks will likely be included in the granite price and will be completed by the granite installer. Likewise, if you'll be installing a bathroom vanity with a pre-fabricated top and sink, the installation will be done by your cabinet installer. In both of these cases, the plumber will still need to hook up the drain line to the new sink, which should cost $40-$60.

12

INSTALL OR REPLACE FAUCETS

Labor: $40-$80

Materials: $20-$200

A typical bathroom faucet will cost $20-$60 and a typical kitchen faucet will cost $80-$200 for low- to mid-level quality.

INSTALL OR REPLACE SHOWER/TUB HARDWARE	**Labor: $40-$150** **Materials: $50-$200** The labor pricing will depend on whether you are just replacing the trim kit or whether the mixer is being replaced as well. If you'll be replacing the mixer as well, the plumber will likely need to cut into the wall behind the tub, which may result in some separate drywall patching. Likewise, the material costs will highly depend on quality of the hardware and whether you are purchasing just a trim kit or a full kit with mixer.
INSTALL OR REPLACE TOILETS	**Labor: $60-$100** **Materials: $100-$200 for each one.**
REPLACE WASHER BOX	**$150-$250**
INSTALL DISHWASHER	**$80-$150**
FIX LEAKS	**$50-$500 for each one.** The cost to fix a leak will depend on how accessible the pipe is, the severity of the leak, and the piping material used. For a typical leak in a supply or drain line, the work should only take an hour or two and will generally cost less than $250. For leaks under the slab where the plumber will need to run a new line above the slab to replace the leaking pipe, expect to pay up to $500. In the case where you have a leak under the slab that must be repaired under the slab, prices could escalate to over $1,000 to find the specific location of the leak, tear up the concrete, and then patch the concrete after fixing the leak. Keep in mind that repairing a leak may require damaging sheetrock, concrete, or cabinets, depending on where the leak is. Factor the cost of repairing any damage into other components.
UNCLOG DRAINS	**$80-$150 for each one.**

12

Determining Your Local Prices

Many plumbers will be willing to give you a ballpark figure for each of these tasks over the phone, though for more complex tasks (like building a custom shower), the contractor will likely want to see the job before throwing out a price. My recommendation is to ask the cost of repiping the house, and if the plumber will throw out a per-fixture price, that's a good sign (especially if it's a good price). If he won't throw out the price for repiping without seeing the job, ask how much he charges to replace a toilet or a faucet—that should give you an idea of whether his other costs will be on the low end or the high end. Keep in mind that most licensed plumbers will be accustomed to doing retail jobs, and will typically charge by the hour, not the task. You may be well served to explain to the plumber your business model and see if they are willing to give you fixed pricing for the common tasks you'll be asking them to do, such as installing sinks, faucets, and toilets.

Plumbers tend to be more expensive than most contractors—they have more formal education and require licenses that many other contractors won't be required to have—so pricing is often much higher than having unlicensed handymen complete the work. It's up to you which way to go, but again, I highly recommend that anyone who is working on plumbing tasks in your property have appropriate licensing and insurance.

How to Pay for the Job

A licensed plumber will typically not require much, if any, of an upfront payment, especially for small jobs. But for large projects that will take place over the course of several weeks—for example, when the plumber has both rough and finish work to do at different phases of the project— he may want payment in several draws .

12

COMPONENT #13
ELECTRICAL

Overview

When you're first starting out, the electrical system of a house can appear to be a complicated and daunting. My goal in this section is to break down the electrical system into its basic components and provide enough detail so that you will have the ability to evaluate those components when creating your SOW and rehab estimate. I'll try not to go into so much detail to put you to sleep while reading.

One word of caution before I continue—electricity is dangerous and many of the electrical components of a house can be deadly if handled improperly. I highly recommend that you don't handle any electrical components in your property if you're not properly trained and understand the risks associated with your actions.

With that disclaimer out of the way, I like to think about it in terms of four basic components to a home electrical system:

1. Service and meter
2. Circuit breaker panel or fuse box
3. Rough wiring
4. Finish electrical

THE SERVICE AND METER

The electricity in a house is supplied by cables coming to the home either overhead or under the ground. Electrical service is measured in terms of voltage (volts) and amperes (amps); if you think of electricity running through a wire as analogous to water running through a pipe, the voltage is analogous to the amount of the *pressure* pushing the water through the pipe and the amperes are analogous to the *volume* of water flowing through the pipe.

In almost all circumstances, the voltage entering a modern house is 240 volts (even though most electrical outlets are 120V outlets) and is provided through three wires coming to the service panel or electrical meter. In some older homes, only two wires are used, bringing in 120 volts. Older, 120-volt service is not powerful enough for most modern-day home needs, and if you ever encounter 120-volt service, you should speak with the local electricity company and a qualified electrician to get the service updated.

The "size" of the electrical service coming into a house is measured in terms of number of amps, which is going to be directly related to the physical size of the wires coming from the electrical cables at the street and into the home—larger wires carry more current. Typical service sizes include 30-amp, 60-amp, 100-amp, and 200-amp, with some areas using other intermediate sizes (125-amp and 150-amp, for example).

Generally speaking, larger service sizes will allow the homeowner to run more and larger appliances simultaneously, without blowing a fuse or tripping a circuit breaker.

Both 30- and 60-amp service are generally considered too small for most modern homes, as central electric air conditioning and some larger appliances will require at least 40-amp service. For a typical 3-bedroom house with standard appliances, 100-amp service is most common.

In larger single-family homes and multi-family properties, 200-amp service is typical. Heat pumps (central electric heating) will generally require their own 100-amp service, with the other 100-amp service used for the rest of the household electrical needs.

When an electrician or contractor refers to "upgrading the service," they are referring to upgrading the size of the service, which involves bringing in larger wires from the electrical cables at the street and potentially upgrading the electrical meter on the exterior of the house. To determine the size of the electrical service in a particular house, look at the circuit breaker or fuse box, which is the next piece of the electrical puzzle.

THE CIRCUIT BREAKER OR FUSE BOX

13

While you may have 100- or 200-amp electrical service coming into the house, most electrical appliances don't require that much amperage in order to operate, and putting high-amp wires (which are larger than lower-amp wires) throughout the house is cumbersome, expensive, and dangerous. This is why a household electrical system brings the main service wires into the house and then distributes that electrical service through the house via smaller lines called circuits. These are the lines that run to each of the outlets in the house.

A fuse box (in older homes) or a circuit breaker panel (in modern homes) is where the main electrical service will be divided into many individual circuits. Circuits will typically range in size from 15 amps to 40 amps, with some larger appliances requiring circuits up to 100 amps in size. Different sized circuits will use different sized wires.

Each circuit attaches to a fuse (if a fuse box is used) or circuit breaker (if a breaker panel is used). The purpose of a fuse or breaker is to cut the electricity to that circuit if the amount of electricity suddenly exceeds the designated circuit size. This can happen when an appliance has a short circuit, for example; by having a fuse or circuit breaker instantly stop the flow of electricity, the appliance won't overheat, start a fire, and burn down the house.

Depending on the size of the circuit and the layout of the house, each circuit will service a particular part of the house, a particular set of outlets, or a particular appliance. If a fuse box or circuit breaker is not rated to support the size of the circuit coming into the house or if the panel isn't physically large enough to support the number of needed circuits, you may have to upgrade the panel and all of the fuses or breakers. And if you're working with a home that has an old fuse box, you may seriously want to consider upgrading to a circuit breaker panel instead.

THE ROUGH WIRING

The rough wiring includes the electrical lines that run from the fuse box or circuit breaker through the walls and to the individual outlets in the house. This wiring is originally run prior to sheetrock going up, but in cases where you are adding a new circuit in an existing property (or even upgrading all the electrical circuits), you may find that you'll need to run wires through an otherwise finished house.

Obviously, running new wires where there is already sheetrock will be more time-consuming and expensive than running wires where there is no sheetrock; additionally, running new wires behind existing sheetrock will result in some minor (if you're lucky) sheetrock damage that will need to be repaired. Keep that in mind when we get to the pricing part of this chapter.

Each circuit will terminate at one or more electrical wall outlets or appliance hook-ups, and if you're finishing a room or adding a new space, you'll likely need at least one or two new circuits to feed the outlets, switches, and lights—or fans in that room. If you are just looking to add a new outlet or two in an existing room, your electrician may be

13

able to wire the new outlets using the existing circuit (just wiring from an existing outlet to the new location), which will generally be a little bit easier and cheaper.

As long as I am discussing electrical outlets, I should discuss those old two-prong outlets that were common in houses prior to the 1980s. These outlets have since been replaced with three-prong outlets that support newer appliances that have three-prong plugs. That third prong on the plug is a grounding line and provides some additional protection to appliances to ensure that they don't short circuit or start a fire. The third prong on the outlet should attach to a grounding wire that runs from the outlet back to the circuit breaker panel and is then grounded at the metal part of the plumbing system or attached to a grounding rod.

Note that a three-pronged plug will *not* provide any additional protection when plugged into a three-prong outlet unless the third prong of that outlet is actually attached to a ground wire. Replacing a two-prong outlet with a three-prong outlet without adding a ground wire will only provide a false sense of protection, and a home inspector will almost certainly find the discrepancy on a typical home inspection.

The other special types of outlets I should mention are called ground-fault interrupter (GFI or GFCI) and arc-fault circuit interrupter (AFCI).

GFCIs are relatively new types of outlets that are very sensitive to even minute differences in electrical current going into and out of the outlet, and when a GFCI detects a current difference, it will immediately interrupt the circuit. GFCIs are now required in all new wiring in kitchens and baths, as water poses an increased risk of accidental electrocution, and a GFCI unit will protect against these types of accidents. The special circuitry can be added either to the breaker or to the outlet.

AFCI is a special circuit breaker designed to prevent fires by detecting unintended electrical arcs and disconnecting the power before a fire starts. AFCI is required in bedrooms and basements by most building authorities. The circuitry is added to the circuit breakers and can be relatively expensive (about $30 per breaker) compared to typical circuit breakers.

These first three electrical components—the service and meter, the circuit breaker panel or fuse box, and the rough wiring—are referred to as the "rough electrical" components of the house, with the "finish electrical" being the piece we discuss next.

13

THE FINISH ELECTRICAL

The finish electrical components consist of all of the electrical components that are visible throughout the house. This includes the lights, fans, outlets and switches, as well as things like the garbage disposal hook-up and bath fan hook-ups.

Replacing finish electrical components doesn't generally require an electrician; a good handyman can generally complete any finish electrical tasks without a problem. That said, when any of your contractors are dealing with electrical components, you probably want to ensure that their insurance is up to date, as even a small mistake when dealing with electrical tasks can result in serious injury. For this reason, I will use a licensed electrician, even for finish electrical tasks—the extra cost is worth it to me in terms of reduced risk and liability.

Inspection Tips

One of the most important aspects of an electrical inspection is verifying the condition of the fuse box or circuit panel. But because of the real risk of injury or death from live electrical circuit, I *never* recommend that you remove the cover from your panel.

In any house you're seriously considering purchasing, you should bring in a qualified electrical contractor or inspector to inspect the fuse box or circuit panel. He can verify that the size of the panel is reasonable for the house, that the panel is wired correctly, and that the components are in working order. It's expensive to upgrade electrical service, so having a qualified contractor or inspector verify these things will help eliminate any major surprises in the budget later in the project.

With that in mind, there are some aspects of the electrical system you can—and should—test yourself during a walkthrough of the property:

13

- Check every electrical fixture, including lights, fans, and appliances. Even if you plan to change out these fixtures, this should give you an idea of whether there are potential wiring issues throughout the house.
- Purchase an outlet tester at your local Home Depot or Lowe's. These devices are inexpensive—under $10—and can be used to verify that outlets throughout the house are wired correctly. You don't need to test every outlet, but you should test a representative sample. If many of the outlets in the house are mis-wired, this can be an indication that there are other electrical issues throughout the house.

- One specific thing to note when testing outlets is whether the three-pronged outlets are grounded correctly. In older houses with original wiring and two-pronged outlets, there was no ground wire run to the outlets. In some cases, homeowners upgrade to three-pronged outlets, but the ground wire wasn't added. This can be a safety hazard and will be flagged by your buyer's inspector and perhaps his lender as well.
- If you plan to do major electrical upgrades, note whether there are GFCI outlets in the kitchens and bathrooms. When you pull permits to upgrade other parts of the electrical system in the house, your building inspector will most likely require the kitchen and bathroom outlets to be upgraded to GFCI at the same time.

Life Expectancy

Each electrical component will have its own life expectancy. The service meter, fuse box, or circuit breaker panel and rough wiring can easily last decades; it is the finish electrical components that are susceptible to the most wear and tear and will deteriorate the fastest. In addition, lights and fans tend to be taste-specific, and as tastes change, these quickly go out of style.

Scope of Work (SOW) Tasks

If you're doing more than just replacing lights and fans, you'll most likely be bundling together a whole bunch of electrical tasks for your electrician to take care of at once. For example, if you're upgrading your service, you'll likely also be upgrading your panel and replacing all the circuit breakers. If you're adding a new circuit, you'll be adding an outlet or appliance to hook up to the circuit. For this reason, your electrician might describe the work in more or fewer steps. But, in general, here are the electrical tasks that are most common on houses you'll be renovating:

13

| SERVICE CALL | Any time an electrician visits your property, he will charge a minimum fee for his time and expertise. This minimum is generally referred to as a "service fee" or "service call fee." |

UPGRADE SERVICE	If you don't have at least 100-amp service, you should seriously consider upgrading your electrical service to either 100 or 200 amps, depending on the size of the house and the appliances that will be run.
REPLACE CIRCUIT PANEL	If your circuit breaker panel doesn't support the size of the service you have (or are upgrading to) or if the panel doesn't have enough physical space to support all the circuits you'll need, you'll likely need to upgrade the panel or add a second panel.
REWIRE HOUSE	Rewiring an entire house is a significant undertaking and the actual amount of work involved will depend on many factors, including: • Size of house. • Number of levels or floors in the house. • Sheetrock or no sheetrock on walls. • Number of outlets, switches, and boxes. • Location of the panel. Rewiring a single-story house that is torn down to the studs (no sheetrock) could cost substantially less than rewiring the same square footage house that is multiple stories, with sheetrock in place. I can provide some very general guidelines for cost, but ultimately, you'll need to get a qualified electrician onsite to look at the job and give you a firm bid.
ADD NEW CIRCUIT	If you'll be finishing a room or adding new electrical service to a part of the house that doesn't currently have electrical service, you'll need to add one or more circuits from the panel.
ADD NEW OUTLET OR BOX	A new outlet or appliance box can be added to an existing circuit by wiring from another outlet in the vicinity, or it can be wired from a new circuit run from the circuit box. Either way, there is cost to cut the drywall opening, add the electrical box, and wire the receptacle (if adding an outlet).
UPGRADE OUTLET TO GFCI	If you'll be doing permitted electrical work, the building inspector will likely require all kitchen and bathroom outlets to be upgraded to GFCI outlets. Even if you don't pull permits or if the inspector doesn't require it, it's a good upgrade to perform for your buyers.

13

ADD NEW SWITCH	If you're adding a new light or fan, you may need to add one or more switches. The wiring for the switches will run from the location of the switch to the location of the appliance being controlled and may involve cutting drywall to run the lines.
INSTALL CAN LIGHT	The cost of installing a new ceiling can light will generally include the wiring from an existing circuit, installation of the rough electrical, installation of the can, and then finishing trim to make the can light look good. Remember, with most new can light installations, you'll generally need at least one new switch.
INSTALL LIGHT	This may involve replacing an existing light or installing a light at a newly installed electrical box.
INSTALL FAN	This may involve replacing an existing fan or installing a fan at a newly installed electrical box.
REPLACE OUTLETS AND SWITCHES	For many of your rehabs, you'll see that the outlets and switches are old and grungy, and it's easier to just replace the receptacle (the actual physical outlet piece) or switch as opposed to trying to clean them.

Cost Guidelines

You may find that if you're doing a lot of electrical work, some of the costs may overlap into more than one area (to reduce the overall cost) or may make it look like one task is more expensive while another task is less expensive. Also, keep in mind that most electricians will charge based on the amount of time they spend, and will have a minimum charge based on at least one hour of work. Since most electricians will charge between $60 and $100 an hour, this is generally the minimum charge. Also note that the prices below may or may not include the cost of obtaining permits. In areas where permits are especially expensive, electricians may pass the actual cost of the permit onto the investor.

13

SERVICE CALL	**$60-$100.**
	If you have an electrician visit your property for any reason, expect to pay for a service call, which typically amounts to the cost of an hour of the electrician's time. So, even if the work you need done only requires ten minutes of work and no materials, you should still expect to pay this minimum fee.
UPGRADE SERVICE	**$1,200-$2,500.**
	This includes upgrading the service to 100 or 200 amps from existing 60-amp service or less. This is a labor and materials price that includes cost of the new meter, the service cable, grounding rods, a new circuit panel (which will almost always be required), and the circuit breakers for the new panel.
	The actual price will be determined by the hourly cost of the electrician, availability of the incoming service wire, and the types of breakers required—some parts of the house may require AFCI breakers, which are relatively expensive.
	If the circumstances aren't ideal—for example, if the incoming electrical service isn't located anywhere near where the circuit panel is located—the cost can be significantly higher. But an electrician will tell you if and why circumstances warrant a much higher cost.
REPLACE CIRCUIT PANEL	**$800-$1,500.**
	This price includes the cost of the new panel (generally between $200-$300), all the new breakers (between $6-$30 each), and the labor involved. If you're upgrading the entire service, this cost should be included in the overall price of the service upgrade.
	Generally, you'll just be upgrading a panel when the existing panel is undersized (not rated for the size of the service you have) or when the panel is physically too small to support the number of circuits/breakers you need.
	Note that adding many AFCI breakers will increase your cost. And, in general, the more breakers you have, the higher the cost will be.

13

REWIRE HOUSE	**$50-$100 per outlet, switch, or fixture.**
	The actual cost of the rewire is going to be highly dependent on the configuration of the house and whether there is sheetrock in the house or not.
	This cost *does not* include the cost of upgrading the service or installing a new circuit panel. (The new panel will likely be required when rewiring.)
	For a typical single-story, 3-bedroom, 2-bath house, expect a total rewire to cost in the ballpark of $5,000-$8,000. For a 2-story house, the price could increase to about $10,000. For larger houses, $10,000-$20,000 is fairly common.
ADD NEW CIRCUIT	**$125-$250 each.**
	The actual cost will depend on the type of breaker that is required (arc fault breakers are often required in bedrooms and basements and can cost up to $30 each) and the length and complexity of the wire run. If you're running wire a short distance from the panel to the location of the outlet or box, the price will be less; if the run is longer, and if the electrician needs to fish the wire through sheetrock and hard-to-reach places, the cost will be more. The cost includes labor and materials, including the electrical box—and if the circuit is for an outlet, the actual outlet and the cover plate. Note that GFCI outlets will add $20-$30 to the cost.
ADD NEW OUTLET	**$60-$100 each.**
	If you want to add a new outlet to an existing circuit (meaning there are likely other outlets nearby), the time and effort to add a new outlet is considerably less than adding a whole new circuit. The cost includes labor and the materials, including the electrical box, the outlet itself, and the cover plate.
	Note that adding GFCI outlets will add $20-$30 to the cost.
UPGRADE OUTLET TO GFCI	**$30-$50 each.**
	The cost of a GFCI outlet itself can range from $10-$20, so a decent portion of this cost is materials alone. While it's just as easy to have your electrician do this work if he is doing other work in the house, a qualified handyman can probably accomplish this task for less money in about the same amount of time.

13

ADD NEW SWITCH	**$100-$150 each.** This cost assumes that the appliance or outlet being controlled is already installed and is relatively close to the switch location. The cost includes labor and the materials, including the electrical box, the switch itself, and the cover plate.
INSTALL CAN LIGHT	**$60-$100 each.** With can lighting, I will generally allow the electrical contractor to provide all materials in addition to the labor. If a new circuit is needed, that will add to the cost, and you should generally factor in the cost of a new switch as well.
INSTALL LIGHT	**Labor: $30-$60.** **Materials: $10 and up.**
INSTALL FAN	**Labor: $40-$70.** **Materials: $20 and up.**
REPLACE OUTLET OR SWITCH	**$5-$10 each.** This price is normally associated with replacing all (or many) outlets and switches throughout a house and including both the labor and the cost of the outlet or switch and the cover plate. Personally, I prefer to have my electrician (or handyman) charge me an hourly rate to replace outlets and switches, as it's normally cheaper this way.

Determining Your Local Prices

Many electricians will be willing to give you a ballpark figure for each of these tasks over the phone, though for more complex tasks (like upgrading the service or replacing the panel), the electrician will likely want to see the job before providing a price. My recommendation is to ask the cost of replacing a light or fan to gauge the price range of the electrician, and if the electrician is competitive on those prices, you can move onto the more complex task pricing when getting bids on an actual job. Keep in mind that most licensed electricians will be accustomed to doing retail jobs, and will typically charge by the hour, not the task. You may be well served to explain to the electrician your business model and see if they are willing to give you fixed pricing for the common tasks you'll be asking them to do, such as installing lights and fans.

Electricians tend to be more expensive than most contractors—they will have more formal education, more insurance, and are in a higher-risk profession than most other contractors—so pricing will often be much higher than having unlicensed handymen complete the work. It's up to you which way to go, but again, I highly recommend that anyone who is working on electrical tasks in your property have appropriate licensing and insurance. Improperly installed wiring can *burn down your house*. Saving a few bucks on a dubious electrician is never worth it.

How to Pay for the Job

A licensed electrician will typically not require much, if any, of an upfront payment, especially for small jobs. But for large projects that will take place over the course of several weeks—for example, when the electrician has both rough and finish work to do at different phases of the project—the electrician may want payment in several draws.

13

COMPONENT #14
HVAC

Overview

A typical heating, ventilation, and air conditioning system (HVAC) will contain three components:

1. Heating system
2. Cooling system
3. Distribution system

HEATING SYSTEM

Contemporary heating systems consists of two main components—the type of fuel they use and the method of distributing the heat. The three major types of fuel in modern-day heating systems is natural gas, electric, and oil. (Solar is less common but growing in popularity. For the purposes of this book, we'll stick with traditional fuels.) For distributing the heat, you'll find that forced air, water, or electrical wiring are most common means of distribution. You can find many combinations of fuel and distribution type, but the most common are the following:

- **Forced Air Units Using Natural Gas or Oil (Furnaces):** This is by far the most common type of system. It consists of a furnace unit that contains a "heat exchanger," which heats air passing over it and then distributes that air via ductwork to the house. The furnace also has an intake that pulls recirculated air back to it, to keep air flowing through the house.

- **Forced Air Units Using Electricity (Heat Pumps):** A heat pump is actually part of the central air conditioning system, but I'm listing it here to be complete. A heat pump works by reversing the process of the air conditioning unit to provide warm air to the house; in most cases, a heat pump doesn't replace a furnace (it's not as powerful as a furnace, and usually isn't used when temperatures get below freezing), but instead is used as an energy and cost-efficient alternative in mild climates or during mild conditions.

- **Radiant Heat Using Gas, Oil, or Electricity (Boilers and Electric):** Radiant heat systems supply heat directly to floors (most common), walls, or ceilings of the house, and that heat is transferred throughout the house as radiant energy. The two most common types of radiant heat are generated by hot water boiler and by electricity. In a hot water radiant heat system, a hot water boiler powered by gas, oil, or electricity heats water and then distributes that water throughout the house via pipes under the floor. In an electrical radiant heat system, electric cables or wires built into floors create radiant heat through electrical resistance. In many cases both hot water and electrical radiant heat systems can be distributed via baseboard units in each room, as opposed to directly under the floor. Unlike forced air furnaces and heat pumps, radiant heat systems require a separate air conditioning system and distribution.

COOLING SYSTEM

Central air conditioning is a common add-on to forced-air furnaces. The air conditioning system has two purposes—to provide cool air through the distribution system and to reduce the amount of humidity in the air. The air conditioning system consists of both an indoor component and an outdoor component:

- **Evaporator Coil (Indoor Component):** The coil sits in the ductwork above the furnace and uses a liquid refrigerant to draw heat out of the air. The warm air "boils" the liquid (reducing the temperature of the air), thus creating gas (which is sent to the outdoor unit) and condensation (the condensation is the humidity taken out of the air). The condensation runs out of the furnace through a pipe, either to outside the house or to an interior drain. Note that this condensation and condensation pipe is a frequent source of water leaks below a furnace.
- **Compressor/Condenser (Outdoor Component):** The compressor is the unit that sits outside the house, and it has the job of turning the refrigerant gas back into liquid by compressing it.

In a heat pump system, the heating is done by reversing the motor in the compressor/condenser to create warm air circulating through the ductwork.

14

There are other forms of air cooling systems, but they are much less common these days.

DISTRIBUTION SYSTEM

The type of distribution system you have will depend on the type of heating and cooling system you have. With a forced air system, the distribution method will consist of ductwork traveling to and from the furnace and the conditioned rooms; ducts will take warm air from the furnace to the rooms and other ducts will return the cool air back to the furnace to create circulation.

Radiant systems use either pipes or wires to distribute the heating elements. In hot water systems, hot water pipes take water from a boiler either through the floor or to baseboard units located throughout the house. And in electric radiant systems, cables or wires are distributed either in the floor or to baseboard units throughout the house.

Furnace and Air Conditioning Compressor Sizing

When purchasing a new furnace or air conditioner, it's important that you purchase a correctly sized unit. Purchasing a unit that is too small will result in a house that takes a long time to heat up or cool down and that can't properly maintain temperature. Purchasing a unit that is too big will unnecessarily eat into your profits and may even be inefficient when it comes to heating and cooling your home.

FURNACE SIZING

Furnaces are measured in two units, output and efficiency:

- **Furnace Output:** Furnace output is measured in British thermal units (BTU). This is the amount of energy that is consumed by the furnace and indicates its heating ability. Most standard furnaces have an output in the 30,000-120,000 BTU range, with higher output furnaces generally costing more than lower output furnaces.
- **Furnace Efficiency:** Furnace efficiency is the percentage of the measure of how much heat is put out by the furnace in relation to the amount of energy it uses. In other words, efficiency measures how well the furnace is able to use the energy it consumes. The lowest legal efficiency for a furnace in the U.S. these days is 78 percent, with the most efficient units at around 97 percent efficiency. Higher efficiency units are more expensive than lower efficiency units but will waste less money on fuel costs.

If you multiply the theoretical output of your furnace by the efficiency, you'll get the actual output that furnace provides. For example, a 60,000 BTU furnace with 90 percent efficiency will have an actual output of

14

54,000 BTUs (60,000 × 90%).

A qualified HVAC professional can give you an idea of the correct sizing for the unit in a specific house (or part of house), or you can find many good online calculators that will help you estimate the correct sized unit. The size will depend upon factors including the square footage, the construction materials of the house, the insulation levels, the number of windows, the size of rooms, and the openness of the floor plan. Some houses will have separate units for each level or for major areas of the house.

Here is a very rough formula you can use to help determine furnace size:

Warmer Climates:
BTU requirement = (square footage of living space) × 25

Cooler Climates:
BTU requirement = (square footage of living space) × 35

Remember, this is just a rule of thumb, and many HVAC contractors would yell at me for even suggesting that you can estimate the furnace size using such a simple calculation. They are probably correct, but I'm a big fan of using rules of thumb to ensure that we at least know what ballpark we're in.

AIR CONDITIONER SIZING
Like furnaces, air conditioning sizing consists of both output and efficiency measures:

- **A/C Output:** Air conditioning output is also measured in BTUs but is commonly converted to a unit called a "ton of refrigeration" (more commonly just called a "ton"). A ton is equivalent to 12,000 BTUs, and most compressors are sized in half-ton increments (1-ton, 1.5-ton, 2-ton, 2.5 ton, etc.)
- **A/C Efficiency:** For air conditioning systems in the United States, energy efficiency is rated by the "seasonal energy efficiency ratio" (SEER). The higher the SEER rating, the more energy efficient the air conditioner. Without going into all the math behind the calculation, the current minimum SEER requirement in the U.S. for central air systems is 13 SEER.

14

Again, a qualified HVAC professional will be able to tell you what the correct size should be for your air conditioning system, but if you're looking for a rule of thumb, here is a formula you can use:

Tons = (square footage of living space) / 500

In other words, 1 ton per 500 square feet of living space.

And again, don't use this rule of thumb to make purchasing decisions—you should listen to what your HVAC professional tells you, as the actual calculation is going to be based on many more factors than just the size of the house.

For more information about correctly sizing HVAC systems, do an internet search for "Manual J Load Calculation." This is the scientific method for calculating furnace sizes that many HVAC professionals use. It uses all the pertinent information about your home, including square footage, construction materials of the house, insulation levels, number of windows, and the size of rooms, to determine an accurate sizing for your HVAC components.

R22 (Freon) Versus R410A Cooling

No discussion of HVAC systems would be complete without touching on an important upcoming change in air conditioning standards. For over 80 years, the standard refrigerant used in cooling systems has been a liquid known as R22—better known by its brand name, Freon.

Due to its negative impact on the environment, R22 will be banned from use starting January 1, 2020. A new refrigerant standard—R410A—has, for the most part, replaced Freon as the refrigerant of choice in the HVAC industry.

Unfortunately, this standards change is having a big impact on anyone who is considering repairing or replacing a cooling system in the next several years.

Here is what you need to know with respect to these changes:

- If you have an exterior air conditioning unit that is R22 based, starting on January 1, 2020, you will no longer be able to make repairs that require the addition of Freon to the system. Freon will not be available after this time, and these units are not compatible with the new R410A standard refrigerant.
- R22 air conditioning units require an evaporator coil that is R22 com-

patible. Likewise, the newer R410A air conditioning units require an evaporator coil that is R410A compatible. If you plan to replace your R22 air conditioning unit with an R410A unit, you will also need to replace the evaporator coil as part of the upgrade. This will typically add a good bit to the cost of an upgrade to your cooling system.

What this means for you is that you should consider the impact of repairing or upgrading the cooling systems in your properties that use Freon. You should also consider the impact of leaving older R22 units in your properties, as your buyers won't have the ability to do relatively simple repairs on these units starting in 2020.

Inspection Tips

Here are some tips on inspecting the HVAC system on any property you're considering:

- First, you should determine whether any of the major components of the HVAC system should be replaced based on age, size, or condition.
- Start your inspection by trying to determine the age of the furnace, boiler, and any exterior AC units. Typically, there is a sticker or plaque attached somewhere on the furnace, compressors, and heat pumps that contains basic information—manufacturer, model number, serial number, etc. In many cases, the date of manufacture will be listed here as well. In some cases, you can glean the year of manufacture from the serial number. If the furnace is more than 18 years old, any compressor is more than 15 years old, any heat pump is more than 12 years old, or the boiler is more than 25 years old, you should either replace it or have it assessed by an HVAC professional to determine if it should be replaced.
- Next, determine the size of the furnace (tons or BTU) and the size of the AC units (tons), and using the rules of thumb mentioned earlier in this section, figure out if the heating and cooling equipment is sufficient for the size of the house and the climate.
- If the exterior air conditioning unit(s) are R22 compatible—again, this should be listed on the sticker or plaque—you should consider whether it would be worthwhile to upgrade the unit and coil to R410A-based equipment. When making this determination, consider the age of the equipment, the condition, and whether you believe this is something a buyer will require in order to complete a sale.
- Best case, every room in the house should have heat and air condition-

14

ing distributed to it, and there should be an air return in each room as well. In reality, this is often not the case, but you should ensure that most rooms are supplied with air and that at least the larger rooms have adequate air returns.

- I recommend turning on the heat as soon as you enter the property. Do this even on a hot day in summer. It sometimes takes a furnace a few minutes to start up, so doing this early in the walk-through will give the unit time to get running and will give you time to see how well the unit is working based on how quickly the property heats up. You should feel hot air coming from each of the supply vents throughout the house.

- While the furnace is running, listen for loud or strange noises and notice if there is unusual vibration. Both of these things can be an indication of furnace issues.

- For properties that have air conditioning units, once you've verified that the heat works, simply set the thermostat to cool. Within a few minutes, you should feel cool air coming from each of the supply vents, and you should feel hot air being expelled from the exterior AC unit.

- If your property has a heat pump, you can test it in similar fashion as the furnace and air conditioning system. That said, note that you should *not* operate a heat pump in cooling mode when the temperature outside is less than 65 degrees and you should *not* operate a heat pump in heating mode when the temperature outside is above 65 degrees.

- For boilers and other electric or water-based heating systems, you can test the heat in a similar fashion as you would a furnace. You will want to ensure that there are enough radiators or baseboard units throughout the property to ensure an even temperature and that all radiators or baseboard units are working properly.

Life Expectancy

The life expectancies for the various HVAC components are as follows:

- Forced air furnace: 20-25 years.
- Air conditioning unit: 15-20 years.
- Heat pump: 10-20 years.
- Hot water boiler: 30-40 years.

Scope of Work (SOW) Tasks

There are many different combinations of the heating and cooling sys-

14

tems, and it would be cumbersome to discuss every task associated with providing and maintaining heating and cooling units. Instead, I will provide the most common tasks (and prices) you'll need to be aware of when dealing with HVAC renovations:

SERVICE CALL	Any time an HVAC professional visits your property, he will charge a minimum fee for his time and expertise. This minimum is generally referred to as a "service fee" or "service call fee."
HVAC MAINTENANCE	Unless I've installed a new HVAC system, I will have my HVAC contractor test the furnace and compressor to ensure everything is working properly, clean the furnace, and check the drip line and other components.
INSTALL FORCED AIR SYSTEM	Installing a new forced air system consists of installing all of the ductwork throughout the house, installing the indoor furnace/coil, and installing an outdoor air conditioning compressor. Depending on the access within the walls and through crawlspaces, attics, and unfinished spaces, this could be a relatively quick and easy job (a day or two) or a very complex and time-intensive job (a week or more). Expect that when installing a new system, there will be damage done to existing sheetrock and may require some reconfiguration of wall cavities and unfinished areas of the house.
REPLACE FURNACE	I will generally replace a furnace if it is over 18 years old or if it is not working properly. While HVAC replacement is relatively expensive compared to other renovation costs, a new HVAC system is a great selling feature for your house. Also, it's important to note that you can often replace a furnace without having to replace the associated air conditioning system, as long as the A/C is still in good, working condition.

14

REPLACE AIR CONDITIONING COMPRESSOR/ CONDENSER	I will generally replace an A/C compressor if it is over 18 years old or if it is not working properly. While HVAC replacement is relatively expensive compared with other renovation costs, it is a great selling feature for your house. Also, it's important to note that you can often replace an A/C unit without having to replace the associated air conditioning system, as long as the furnace is still in good, working condition. That said, expect that if you have to replace the outdoor A/C unit, you'll likely need to replace the indoor component (the evaporator coil) as well, as the two work together and must be compatible.
REPLACE HEAT PUMP	If you want to provide some energy efficiency to your rehab and don't mind spending a little extra money, a heat pump can be a great selling feature, especially if you need to replace the air conditioning unit anyway.
REPLACE BOILER	Because boilers are becoming much less common these days, and because prices for boilers are very difficult to determine without more detail about the specific installation, I'm going to avoid calling out estimates for boiler replacement costs.

Cost Guidelines

Because there are so many different brands, sizes, efficiencies, and types of HVAC equipment, generalizing materials prices is difficult. But, here are some general guidelines:

SERVICE CALL	**$60-$100.** If you have a HVAC professional visit your property for any reason, expect to pay for a service call, which typically amounts to the cost of an hour of the electrician's time. So, even if the work you need done only requires ten minutes of work and no materials, you should still expect to pay this minimum fee.

14

HVAC MAINTENANCE

$150-$200.

If you're having any other significant work done on the HVAC system, you can generally negotiate standard maintenance into the cost, but otherwise, you'll pay a flat fee for routine checking and maintenance of the existing system.

Many larger HVAC companies will advertise special pricing for first-time customers, especially just before summer starts. This may be a great opportunity to save some money.

INSTALL FORCED-AIR SYSTEM

$5,000-$8,000.

This price includes a split system (indoor furnace, indoor coil, and outdoor air conditioning unit) plus all the ductwork and wiring installed throughout a typical 1,500-2,000 square foot house.

Materials and installation for a lower end 24-ton, medium-efficiency furnace, coil, and compressor will run about $3,500-$5,000, with the installation of the ductwork running another $1,500-$3,000, depending on the size of the house, the accessibility of ductwork locations, etc.

REPLACE FURNACE

$1,000-$2,000.

Materials for a lower end, natural gas, 70,000 BTU, 80% efficiency furnace run about $700-$800 retail (likely less for your HVAC contractor), and the cost of a lower end, natural gas, 115,000 BTU high-efficiency (96%) furnace run about $1,500-$1,600 retail.

Installation time for a typical install will be four to eight hours.

REPLACE A/C COMPRESSOR AND EVAPORATOR COIL

$1,200-$2,000 for compressor/condenser.

$1,800-$3,000 for compressor/condenser and evaporator coil.

Materials for a lower end, electric, 2-4-ton, 13 SEER air outside conditioning unit run about $700-$1,200 retail (likely less for your HVAC contractor). Materials for a lower end, 2-4-ton evaporator run about $200-$600 retail.

Installation time for a typical install will be four to eight hours.

14

REPLACE HEAT PUMP	**$2,000-$3,500.**
	Materials for a lower end, electric, 2-4-ton, 13 SEER electric heat pump run about $1,500-$2,000 retail (likely less for your HVAC contractor).
	Installation time for a typical install will be four to eight hours.

Determining Your Local Prices

If you need to replace a major HVAC component (boiler, furnace, compressor), a call to a few local HVAC companies should get you some quick and easy estimates, especially if you know the size and efficiency of the unit you're looking for. Many HVAC companies will quote you a price for the more expensive brands, so always ask, "Do you supply another brand with the same characteristics at a lower price?" Often, you'll find that you can get the same type of equipment for a much lower price just by going with a less recognized brand. The prices here reflect the costs of the lower-end brands.

How to Pay for the Job

I always pay for HVAC work at the completion of the job when working with a licensed and reputable HVAC company. When working with an independent contractor (perhaps a retired HVAC professional who does some part-time work or an installer for a larger company working "off the books"), I'll sometimes pay for materials upfront and all labor costs when the job is completed.

14

COMPONENT #15
FRAMING

Overview

When it comes to new construction, framing costs are often the most expensive component of the building process. There are many different materials that can be used for exterior or interior framing, but wood is by far the most common. In this section, we'll cover the two most common costs associated with framing: finishing an interior space and building new construction.

FINISHING AN INTERIOR SPACE

If you'll be finishing an unfinished space or just adding partitions within rooms, you'll want to be familiar with the process of framing a wall. Once you're familiar with the basic process, it will help you estimate the materials and labor that will be required to finish the interior space.

A basic wall consists of three parts:

1. A 2x4 piece of lumber running horizontally along the bottom of the wall. This is called the bottom plate.
2. Two 2x4 pieces of lumber running horizontally along the top of the wall—the top plates.
3. 2x4 pieces of lumber running vertically every 16"—the studs.

In its most basic form, a wall requires three times the length of the wall in lumber for the plates (since you have three plates) and the length of the wall in inches, divided by 16, for the number of studs.

[NOTE: Some of you more familiar with construction will probably note that only load-bearing walls need two top plates, and non-load-bearing walls only need one. But, many framers consider it good practice to always use two top plates.]

As an example, let's say you wanted to build a wall 20' in length (240") and 8' high. You would need:

- 60' of 2x4 lumber (20' × 3)
- 15 pieces of 2x4 lumber, each 8' long (240" / 16)

Add in a box of nails and it should be pretty easy to calculate the amount and cost of material you'd need for this project.

FRAMING A HOUSE

If you'll be building new construction or building an addition that requires new exterior walls, the process is quite a bit more complicated than just estimating the labor and material costs of building the walls. When framing an addition or new build, you are not just building walls but also building floor systems, roofing systems, porches and overhangs, and more. Estimating the cost of such a large undertaking is complex, and even experienced framing contractors will use rough estimating techniques to determine the scope and cost of a particular job.

Oftentimes, the cost of framing will be determined by the square footage of the space being built—a 3,000-square-foot house will cost about twice as much as a 1,500-square-foot house. That said, some framers will charge differently for living space versus non-living-space, such as garages and porches. Some framers will include roof decking and exterior wall sheathing in their bids, and some won't. Some framers will include installation of doors and windows in their bids, and some won't.

Don't expect apples-to-apples comparisons when it comes to framing bids—you'll need to do some legwork to determine how multiple bids compare to one another. Even the amount of material required for the job will often create disagreements among framing contractors; one contractor may estimate 800 2x4 pieces of lumber for a job while another estimates 1,000 2x4s. The differences can add up.

Inspection Tips

Inspecting framing is beyond the scope of this text. Framing codes vary around the country, and for any load-bearing framing members there are many structural considerations that must be considered. If you have any concerns about potentially load-bearing framing members, I highly recommend that you consult a licensed engineer before proceeding with the project.

Life Expectancy

Framing should last the life of the structure.

15

Scope of Work (SOW) Tasks

When doing a renovation you're likely to either need to frame interior walls or frame an entire house or addition. While there are certainly other cases, once you understand the costs behind those two tasks, you should be able to estimate the costs for the related tasks:

FRAME WALLS	If you'll be finishing a basement or unfinished area, or building a partition wall, you will want to use the linear footage of the wall to determine the overall labor and materials cost.
FRAME HOUSE	When framing an entire house, make sure you have a qualified framing crew that specializes in house framing. When estimating costs, your estimate will be based on the square footage of the interior of the structure.

Cost Guidelines

Here's a breakdown of labor and materials for each of these two tasks:

FRAME WALLS	**Labor: $6-$12 per linear foot.**
	Materials: $5-$8 per linear foot.
	Material cost will be dependent on the current cost of lumber, which can vary greatly in different parts of the country and at different times.

15

| FRAME HOUSE | **Labor: $4-$12 per square foot.** |
| | **Materials: $6-$12 per square foot.** |

The price for house framing is going to be tremendously dependent on the location of the project and the current costs of lumber. Because so much lumber is required to frame a large structure, even small variations in lumber prices can impact the overall cost of the project.

Note that if you're building in a high-priced area like California or New York City, your labor costs could be double or triple the range I present here. I've heard of rehabbers in the San Francisco area spending upwards of $40 per square foot on framing labor costs.

Determining Your Local Prices

Lumber prices will often play a large role in defining the cost of framing. Over the past several years, lumber prices have been all over the board, and when lumber prices double, your framing costs can increase 25 percent of more. The best way to determine lumber prices is to visit your local lumberyard or even a typical big-box store. For labor prices, many carpenters will give you an estimate for wall framing without a specific job, though the actual cost will depend on the details of the particular job. A framing contractor for new construction may give you a ballpark per-square-foot figure but won't give a hard quote until he sees the final construction plans.

How to Pay for the Job

Be prepared to pay for (and perhaps even provide) materials upfront. Labor payment can be negotiated, but I prefer to pay either in installments (for large jobs) or at completion of the work (for smaller jobs).

15

COMPONENT #16
INSULATION

Overview

There are several places around your house where insulation will be required by local building codes, and there will be other areas around the house where—especially in cold and hot climates—insulation will be recommended, even if not required.

Typical places where insulation is required are:

- Between studs within wall cavities, especially along exterior walls.
- In an unfinished attic space.
- Within floors over unheated spaces.
- Along unfinished, exposed basement walls.
- Along exterior walls (beneath siding) or under the roof membrane.

The ability for a particular material to insulate is measured using a unit called "R-value." As an example, if one inch of a particular material had an R-value of three (R-3), six inches of that same material would have an R-value of 18 (R-18).

So, if building codes call for an insulation level of R-24 in a certain location, you could use six inches of an insulating material with an R-4 value, you could use two inches of an insulating material that has an R-12 value, or you could even use 24 inches of an insulating material that has an R-1 value.

There are several forms of insulation that are common today:

- Loose fill
- Batt or blanket
- Rigid board
- Foam

LOOSE FILL

Loose fill insulation is just small pieces of fiberglass or cellulose that can be poured or blown into irregular and hard-to-reach areas. It's good for adding insulation into already finished spaces—for example, pouring into the cavities behind a sheetrocked wall. It's also good for unfinished attic spaces, where it can be blown throughout the space using a machine.

Loose fill insulation generally has an R-value between R-2 and R-4 per inch.

BATT OR BLANKET

Batt or blanket insulation comes in rolls that are cut to desired lengths. Widths are typically the standard spacing of wall studs, floor joists, attic trusses, etc. Batt insulation is generally made from fiberglass and is most commonly installed in spaces between studs, joints, and beams. This is the type of insulation most commonly found between the studs in exterior walls and between the floor joists under floors.

Batt insulation generally has an R-value between R-3 and R-4 per inch of thickness.

RIGID BOARD

Rigid board insulation comes in sheets made of polystyrene or polyurethane. The sheets are generally 4' × 8' in size and have some strength to them, making it easy to attach to solid surfaces. Rigid board is thin (less than 1" thick), making it ideal to place behind siding or beneath roof membranes. It's also a popular choice for insulating unfinished basements by just attaching it directly to the foundation wall.

Rigid board insulation generally has an R-value of about R-5 per inch.

FOAM

Foam insulation is a liquid insulation that hardens after application. It can be sprayed or even injected into cavities through small holes. Foam insulation is expensive, but generally has a high R-value (about twice that of batt insulation), making it a great insulating material. Foam is made of polyurethane or other materials, including some that are water soluble.

Foam insulation generally has an R-value up to R-6.5 per inch.

Inspection Tips

The bulk of the insulation in your property will be hidden behind walls, in the ceiling, and in the floor. And unless you'll be opening up walls, you'll probably never know for certain the existence of or the condition of the insulation. Unless I'm concerned about mold behind a wall or have a specific reason to question whether the insulation needs to be replaced in a property, I won't bother taking any drastic steps to check the hidden insulation.

16

The most important place to inspect insulation in most houses is the attic. This is because:

1. More heat escapes through the attic than any other part of the house; and

2. Any decent inspector will check for appropriate attic insulation when your buyer has his inspection.

When inspecting attic insulation, you should be looking for a few things. First, be aware of any areas of the attic that have uneven amounts of, or missing, insulation. Most attic insulation is loose fill, so a visual inspection can typically give you a good idea of whether the attic is evenly insulated or not.

While your local codes may vary, you will generally want an unheated attic to have an R-value of at least R-30 with R-50 to R-60 being even better, especially in colder climates. Given that most loose fill insulation has an R-value of about R-3, this translates to between 10" and 20" of loose fill insulation in your attic.

If the insulation in the attic is something other than loose fill, you should try to determine the R-value of that insulation and figure out if it is adequate or not. If there are multiple types of insulation in the attic, multiply the R-value of each by the thickness and add them together to get the total R-value.

Note that a good installation of insulation in the attic will include a vapor barrier between the floor and the insulation. A vapor barrier is simply a thin layer of sheathing—typically a thin plastic sheet—which keeps moisture from penetrating into the attic and insulation. If the insulation in the attic is moist or damp, you should attempt to determine the source of the moisture and you should seriously consider replacing the wet insulation.

For houses that have unfinished or partially finished basements, you should check to see if the basement walls are insulated. If you plan to finish the basement, you will need to factor in the cost of any new insulation to your scope of work. Most jurisdictions will require basement wall R-values of between R-13 and R-19, again depending on your local climate.

Life Expectancy

If not overly disturbed, most insulation should last the lifetime of the structure.

16

Scope of Work (SOW) Tasks

All insulation tasks will involve the installation of insulation:

INSTALL INSULATION

Different forms of insulation are measured in different ways, so there is no easy way to compare the price of one type of insulation versus another. But different insulation forms each have their common uses, and if you choose the appropriate form for your need, you'll likely get the best value.

While you can have other contractors (handyman, carpenter, sheetrocker) do the work, for large insulation jobs, you'll find that it's more cost effective to have a professional insulation company complete the task.

Loose-fill insulation is generally used for insulating attics and is measured per square foot.

Batt insulation is used for insulating wall cavities and is sometimes used to insulate attics and is measured per linear foot.

Rigid board insulation is used to insulate exterior and unfinished basement walls and is measured in square feet (but installed in 4' × 8' sheets).

Foam insulation is used for high-end properties to insulate wall cavities or for hard-to-reach spaces and is measured in square feet.

Cost Guidelines

Here's the breakdown of costs to install insulation:

INSTALL INSULATION

Loose fill: $1-$2 per square foot.

Batt: $1-$2 per linear foot.

Rigid board: $1-$2 per square foot.

Spray foam: $2-$5 per square foot.

For most applications in low- to mid-level renovations, loose fill and batt insulation will be the insulation of choice.

16

Determining Your Local Prices

Most professional insulation companies will be happy to give you a ball-park figure for large-scale jobs, such as insulating all the exterior walls or blowing insulation in the attic. They'll want to see the job before committing to a price, but you should be able to get an estimate of what your local prices are by making a few phone calls.

How to Pay for the Job

I will typically pay for insulation work at the completion of the job. Some contractors may require a down payment or payment for materials upfront before they get started.

16

COMPONENT #17
SHEETROCK

Overview

Sheetrock is a great building material. It's cheap, easy to work with, and it's durable when treated with care. Small sheetrock patches can be accomplished by many different contractors, and large sheetrock jobs can be completed very efficiently by specialty contractors who sheetrock day in and day out.

The basic process of installing or repairing sheetrock has three steps:

1. **Hanging:** This involves nailing or screwing the sheetrock to the studs of the house until the desired surface area is covered. Sheetrock comes in large sheets that are either 4' × 8' or 4' × 12' and is installed from the top down (ceiling first, then top of walls, then bottom of walls). Holes are cut where there are outlets, switches or other cut-outs, and metal pieces are installed at the corners to ensure clean and smooth right angles.

2. **Taping and mudding:** Once the sheetrock is hung, there will be small spaces between the sheets and there will be indentations where the nails or screws went into the sheetrock. Special sheetrock tape will be used to cover and transition the long cracks between sheets, and then several layers of sheetrock "mud" (much like the consistency of toothpaste) will be used to smooth the tape and fill the indentations.

3. **Sanding and finishing:** Once the mud is dry, it's sanded down to make it smooth and additional mud compound is used to taper the seams and make the transition between sheets imperceptible.

Sheetrock installation and finishing generally take at least three days, and if conditions aren't perfect (for example, cold temperatures or high humidity), the time can easily turn into a week or two. In fact, sheetrock is probably the most difficult renovation task to schedule, as many factors will contribute, and you generally won't know how long the process will take until it's completed.

In some areas around the country, it is standard to apply a "texture" to sheetrock prior to painting. This texture adds an aesthetic value to the finish that many homeowners like. To determine if a texture is appropriate for your renovation, I would recommend looking at competing houses in your market and seeing if the walls in those houses are smooth (no texture) or have a texture applied.

The big advantage to doing texture (in places where it is standard) is that when texture is applied to finished sheetrock, it covers up any imperfections in the wall. Texture can cover up everything from small nail holes to a poor taping or mudding job by the installers. In fact, when I'm installing sheetrock in places where texture is standard, I will expect that the cost of sheetrock installation is actually less expensive, as the coat of texture that will be added will mean that the installers will not need to be as precise as if we were leaving the walls smooth.

While so far this discussion has focused on sheetrock for standard interior walls, there are actually many different types of sheetrock that have other less common uses. Here are a few of the most common types of sheetrock other than standard wallboard:

- **Greenboard:** This is water resistant sheetrock material used in locations with high humidity, such as around tubs and showers. This type of sheetrock is not completely water resistant or mold resistant, but it can withstand more moisture than standard sheetrock.
- **Cement board:** This type of sheetrock is made with thin layers of cement, and is ideal for areas that will be tiled, as the mortar used for the tile will adhere better to the heavy-duty cement board than to standard sheetrock.
- **Fire resistant:** This is sheetrock that can withstand flames for long periods of time without being destroyed. It is typically used in attached garages to create a firewall between the garage and the living space.
- **Insulated:** This type of sheetrock is used in areas that are not well insulated, and it can withstand more moisture than standard sheetrock without warping or deteriorating.

Inspection Tips

When inspecting sheetrock, there are two things you should be looking for:

- **Cosmetic condition.** Most sheetrock work is based on cosmetic defects. You want to ensure that the walls are not bowed, that the tape and mud is evenly distributed and not lumpy, that all nail holes are mudded, and

17

there are no protruding nails. And, of course, you want to ensure that you note any sheetrock damage, such as gouges or holes.

- **Smells.** The other aspect of sheetrock inspection that many investors don't spend enough time investigating is smells. Because sheetrock is porous, it can capture smells like cigarette smoke and animal urine. For sheetrock that has been exposed to these types of odors for long periods of time, it can be very difficult—or even impossible—to remove the smell. I've seen plenty of situations where it was more cost effective to tear out and replace sheetrock than to try to cover it up with primer, paint, or some other type of odor-reducing agent.

Life Expectancy
Sheetrock will last decades unless damaged by impact or moisture.

Scope of Work (SOW) Tasks
When it comes to sheetrock, there are only four things you'll ever need to do:

PREP SHEETROCK FOR PAINT	Painters are accustomed to doing minor prep work on the sheetrock prior to painting. This includes filling in nail holes, smoothing sheetrock that was ripped or torn when fixtures were removed, and patching minor holes. But in some situations, the sheetrock throughout the house is in bad shape, and a significant amount of prep work is required prior to starting painting.
	In these cases, you can either bring in a specialty sheetrock contractor to prep the walls or you can have your painters do it. Personally, I prefer to use my painters, as they are well qualified to do most sheetrock repair and can complete prep work faster than a sheetrock contractor can. But, if your painters can't handle the job—or if the damage is such that large sections of sheetrock need to be removed and replaced—you may want to consider hiring a specialty crew to prepare the walls for painting.
	With two or three qualified workers, a typical 1,500-square-foot house should be able to be prepped in a day, though major prep work or prepping larger houses could take up to two or three days just based on the volume of sheetrock that needs to be examined and touched up.

17

PATCH SHEETROCK

A sheetrock patch consists of installing a piece of sheetrock that is smaller in size than a full sheet. For a typical renovation, you may have several sheetrock patches throughout the house. Unless your sheetrock patches are especially large or there are several dozen of them, you probably don't need a specialty contractor to complete the work.

I will generally have my carpenter, painter, or handyman do sheetrock repairs prior to painting. If my painters will be doing a lot of prep work prior to painting, I'll let them do the sheetrock patching as part of their prep.

Small sheetrock patches can generally be completed in a day, though larger patches will require more time for the mud to dry and will require more time to sand and finish, so you may be looking at two or three days for those to be completed.

INSTALL NEW SHEETROCK

If you need to install a significant amount of new sheetrock (for example, if you're finishing an unfinished space or if you had to remove a lot of moldy sheetrock), you'll want to use a contractor who specializes in sheetrock installation. Because sheetrock is big, bulky, and heavy, sheetrock contractors will generally have processes and equipment to get the sheetrock from the supplier to the appropriate parts of the house. This is the type of work for which non-specialty contractors will charge you extra.

Specialty sheetrock companies will often use different professionals to do different parts of the job—they'll have workers who specialize in hanging the sheetrock, others who specialize in taping and mudding the sheetrock, and perhaps even another crew who does the sanding and finishing.

APPLY TEXTURE

There are many different types of wall textures, and the look and cost will be highly correlated to how the texture is applied. Some textures must be applied by hand and are intricate-looking and costly; other textures are applied by machine and are uniform and inexpensive.

Texture may be applied by the sheetrock contractors if new sheetrock is being hung or may be applied by painters during their prep work.

Cost Guidelines

The following are guidelines for the cost of doing sheetrock work:

PREP SHEETROCK FOR PAINT	**$0-$500.** It's very difficult to determine the cost for prep work on a particular house without actually observing the condition first hand. For a typical house without any significant sheetrock damage, the prep work will be rolled into the painting price, and there will be no additional cost. But if there is significant work required to get the sheetrock in shape for painting, your contractors will likely charge you based on the time they will spend doing the prep and the cost of the prep materials. On a typical 3/2 house, the worst-case number shouldn't be more than $500 for wall prep. If you're facing more than $500 in prep work, it's likely that you need some major sheetrock patching or may even need to have large sections of sheetrock replaced, both of which are covered next.
PATCH SHEETROCK	**$0-$500.** It's very difficult to estimate the cost of sheetrock repair. A very small job (patching a single hole, for example) can cost as much as installing an entire sheet of sheetrock, as the contractor will probably charge a minimum amount just to drive to the site and do the work. If the contractor(s) doing the repairs are already onsite (for example, if your painters are doing your sheetrock repair), expect to pay about $20 per sheetrock patch, as a typical patch will require a few dollars' worth of materials and then about an hour of time. Just like with the prep work above, if you are facing more than $500 in prep work, you will probably be better off consulting with a specialty sheetrock contractor.

17

INSTALL NEW SHEETROCK	**$1.00-$1.50 per square foot of sheetrock used for standard wallboard.**
	Add 10 percent for large areas of non-wallboard such as greenboard or cement board.
	Add 10 percent to the total estimate to account for waste.
	Installing new sheetrock over large areas (more than 1,000 square feet) is much more cost efficient than doing individual sheetrock patches. While per-square-foot pricing is typical for large sheetrock jobs, many sheetrock contractors will charge by the sheet—with typical sheets being either 4' × 8' (32 square feet) or 4' × 12' (48 square feet) in size, you should expect to pay somewhere in the $30-$60 per sheet range using that pricing model.
	Many sheetrock companies will provide all labor and materials for larger jobs (this is how I prefer to do it), but others will expect you to provide the sheetrock and will quote just a labor price. A sheet of sheetrock will generally cost between $10-$14, depending on thickness and size, and extra materials (screws, tape, mud) will generally run about $2-$4 per sheet.
	That means you are looking at $12-$16 per sheet for materials ($.35-$.50 per square foot), and labor will typically run about $18-$25 per sheet ($.60-$.85 per square foot).
	Note that the cost of installing new sheetrock *does not* include the cost of removing and disposing of old sheetrock. This cost should be accounted for as part of the demo phase.
APPLY TEXTURE	**$.05-$.25 per square foot of sheetrock space.**
	Spray-on texture such as "knockdown" or "orange peel" is inexpensive compared to techniques that require your contractor to apply texture by hand using a brush, knife, or other manual tool. Some hand-applied textures are time-consuming and require skill and can cost hundreds of dollars per room to apply.

Determining Your Local Prices

For prep work and sheetrock patches, you will likely be using painters or other non-specialty sheetrock contractors, and they will likely need

17

to evaluate each job individually to determine an appropriate price. In general, if you are spending more than $500 for sheetrock work, you should seriously consider bringing in a specialty contractor.

To determine whether a specialty sheetrock contractor has reasonable pricing, you can generally ask for ballpark pricing to hang and finish 50 sheets. Make sure you are clear about whether the prices include labor and materials or labor-only and also make it clear that you expect the sheetrock to be ready to be painted.

How to Pay for the Job

For patching and prepping, the bulk of the cost is labor, and I pay when the job is complete. For large sheetrock jobs, I will pay for materials up-front and labor at completion of the job.

COMPONENT #18
CARPENTRY—DOORS, WINDOWS, TRIM

Overview

Carpentry can make or break a house. Great carpentry makes a house feel well put together, while poor carpentry will make a buyer question every part of the renovation. A good carpenter can serve in many different roles and can replace a lot of other contractors.

But other than framing and decks, the bread and butter of carpentry work consists of things like door installations, window installations, and finish trim work. These are renovation tasks you'll likely have to perform in every one of your houses, so find a good carpenter sooner rather than later, and you'll find your renovations going more quickly and more smoothly than you can imagine. Bring in a bad carpenter, and all you'll find is lots of frustration and a questionable looking renovation.

In this section, we'll discuss the bread-and-butter carpentry tasks:

- Install doors
- Install windows
- Finish trim

Inspection Tips

When inspecting the carpentry around a property, your two main goals are to ensure functionality and aesthetics.

In terms of functionality, you will want to ensure that every door and every window works properly and as expected. For doors, I will verify the following:

- Does the door open and close without obstruction?
- Does the door latch properly without unnecessary force?
- Does the door open in the expected direction?

For exterior doors, I will do an additional inspection to ensure to that there is no rot or damage on the outside facing side of the door or around the casing/trim.

For each window, I will verify the following:

- Does it open smoothly and easily?
- Does it remain open without assistance?
- Does it close and latch without any unnecessary force.
- Are the panes of glass free from cracks and moisture?
- Are there any gaps or openings around the window?

Life Expectancy

Good carpentry should last as long as the structure lasts.

Scope of Work (SOW) Tasks

The following are the basic carpentry tasks you'll perform on many of your renovations:

BASIC CARPENTRY	There are many tasks on a renovation that a good carpenter can perform. In fact, I like to think of my carpenter as a jack of all trades and will let him do not only all the wood-related work but also all the stuff that I don't want to hire a specialty carpenter for. For example, my carpenter will mount the microwave, install my appliances, help mount mirrors in the bathrooms, install the backsplash behind the kitchen counters, and install all my doorknobs and mini-blinds.
	While my handyman can do a lot of these tasks, my carpenter only costs a little bit more, and his work will generally be cleaner than my handyman's. The other nice thing about using a carpenter for these types of tasks is that if and when he runs into an issue, he's likely more equipped to come up with a creative solution than most of my other contractors.

INSTALL DOORS	If the existing doors are old or beat up, I will often replace all the doors in a house. When purchasing doors, you have the option of purchasing just the door slab (the part that opens and closes) or a pre-hung door (the slab attached to the doorjamb). While many investors are happy to save a little money by just buying the slab, replacing a slab instead of the entire jamb can be more work for your carpenter, and you'll often end up paying extra to fix doors that aren't plumb or don't lock properly. I highly recommend that when replacing a door, you pay the few extra bucks to get a pre-hung door. Your carpenter will appreciate it and you'll save yourself some headaches, even if it costs a bit more.
REPLACE WINDOWS	Windows come in all different shapes, sizes, and styles, and I would highly recommend you spend some time looking at different types of windows and getting a feel for the style of windows that are typical in the houses you plan to renovate.
FINISH TRIM	Finish trim generally includes the following: • Baseboard and shoe molding • Crown molding • Door casing • Window casing

Cost Guidelines

Here are some general guidelines for carpentry costs:

BASIC CARPENTRY	**$25-$35 per hour.** A good carpenter isn't cheap but given that great carpentry can sell a house and bad carpentry can keep you from selling a house, he is worth every penny. If your carpenter has an apprentice, expect to pay between $15-$20 per hour for the apprentice's time, depending on how skilled he is.

18

INSTALL DOOR

EXTERIOR DOOR

Labor: $100-$175.

Materials: $150-$300.

INTERIOR DOOR

Labor: $30-$50.

Materials: $40-$90.

FRENCH DOOR

Labor: $150-$200.

Materials: $300-$600.

SLIDING GLASS DOOR

Labor: $150-$250.

Materials: $300-$600.

A good carpenter can install an exterior door in about an hour, an interior door in about 20 minutes, and a French or sliding glass door in two to three hours. As you can see, the hourly rate a carpenter charges to install doors is quite high; but nonetheless, many carpenters will quote prices even higher than what I list here.

REPLACE WINDOWS

Labor: $750-$1100.

Materials: $100-$200.

Standard double-hung replacement windows come in a variety of sizes, styles, and qualities, but for most low- to mid-level renovations, I would recommend using stock vinyl windows that can be purchased from a big-box store or ordered though a local window company.

You'll likely find that using the window company to install the windows will cost quite a bit more than having a carpenter do the installation. My best suggestion for window installation is to find a professional window installer who is looking for side work at night or on the weekends and pay him an hourly rate for installation. Professional installers can replace a window very quickly and paying hourly will keep the per-window price to a minimum.

FINISH TRIM	Labor: $1.00-$1.50 per square foot.
	Materials: $.75-$1.50 per linear foot.

Notice that the labor cost is based on square footage of the house while material cost is based on the linear feet of actual trim to be installed.

To trim out a full house, many carpenters will charge based on the square footage of the house as opposed to the specific amount of trim you plan to use. So, you may pay the same price regardless of whether you put crown molding in every room or none of them.

These prices are typical for medium to large jobs that will take several days or more, such as trimming an entire house. For smaller jobs, you can base the labor price off the hourly price of your carpenter.

Determining Your Local Prices

Depending on whether your carpenter charges by the hour or by the task will ultimately determine what you're paying for a job (by the hour is often cheaper is if your carpenter is reliable and works diligently). Because a carpenter's job will be pretty diverse on a particular day, until you actually sit down and work through a specific SOW, it will hard to determine the price for individual tasks.

For example, one carpenter might take 15 minutes to install an interior door and another might take 30 minutes. If they were to charge by the task, the prices for each would likely be pretty close. But if they charged hourly, the slower carpenter would cost about twice as much. Therefore, it would seem like an hourly wage is better. But each project will have its challenges, and if a big challenge comes up that requires a large amount of time to fix, paying an hourly wage could end up being the more expensive option. There are risks and trade-offs with each method, though I tend to prefer to get a fixed price bid on each job based on the specific list of tasks.

How to Pay for the Job

Carpenters tend to be on the job for relatively long periods of time, so paying them on a weekly basis, or after completing certain milestones, is how payment is typically handled. You should be prepared to provide all material, though a good carpenter will have connections to local lumber yards and supply houses and should be able to get most of the material delivered directly to the project.

COMPONENT #19
INTERIOR PAINTING

Overview

Interior painting covers the painting of three major components of the interior property:

- Walls
- Ceiling
- Trim

It is most common to use a three-color interior paint scheme: one color for walls, one for the ceiling, and one for the trim. For rehab properties, I highly recommend maintaining a neutral and non- "taste specific" color scheme, with the walls being some variation of beige or gray, the ceiling being a typical "ceiling white," and the trim being a semi-gloss bright white.

While this paint scheme won't excite your buyers, it won't turn them off, which is what you are going for when it comes to paint.

The cost of interior painting will vary based on several factors:

- Prep work required.
- Size of job (square footage).
- Number of coats of paint and primer.
- Complexity of job (intricacy of detail).
- Difficulty of job (heights or difficult to reach locations).
- Type of paint chosen.

I will assume that the bulk of the prep work required to begin painting was already completed during the sheetrock phase of the project, but generally speaking, painters will expect to have to do some wall prep as part of their job.

The big factor that will impact the cost of the job (besides the square footage) will be the number of coats of paint that are required. One thing to keep in mind is that if you have any new sheetrock in the house, that sheetrock will need to be primed prior to being painted. This extra time and cost of priming new sheetrock can add up to 35 percent to the total cost of painting those areas. Additionally, going from a dark color to a light color (or vice-versa) will add an extra coat of paint or primer, so for those types of drastic color changes, be prepared to pay 25 percent extra, or more.

Here are some very general figures that will factor into interior paint pricing. Don't use this as a direct pricing formula, but this should help you get your head around where the costs are coming from:

- A typical mid-grade quality paint will cost about $15-$25 per gallon when purchased by a paint contractor in relatively large quantities. Expect to pay about 50 percent-100 percent more if you're purchasing the paint yourself in smaller quantities.
- A gallon of paint will cover about 400 square feet of wall or ceiling space, which is about the square footage of a 10' × 10' room.
- For a typical investor-quality painter, materials will run about 25 percent of the total cost of the project.
- One coat of paint will be sufficient for well-maintained interior walls, but if you're painting new sheetrock, going from light-to-dark or dark-to-light colors, or if the walls are in bad shape, expect an extra coat of paint and/or primer, which will add 25 percent-35 percent to the cost of the job.

Inspection Tips

It should be pretty obvious if a house needs new interior paint. We will typically paint every house that we renovate, whether we think it needs it or not.

But, if you're considering whether to paint a house or not, here are a few questions to ask yourself:

- Are the current color choices neutral and complementary? Most buyers like neutral colors, as well as colors that work well together. Best case, the buyers don't even notice the paint in the house. If you have walls that stand out because of their color scheme, you should seriously consider new paint.
- Does the paint look fresh and do the walls look clean and smooth? If there are marks on the walls, paint streaks, chipping paint, or if the paint looks dull and old, buyers will notice. And this will be an indication that you've cut corners on your renovation.
- Fresh paint is one of the most inexpensive ways to freshen up an entire house, and the smell of fresh paint will evoke the idea of "clean and new" as your potential buyers walk the house.

Life Expectancy

A good interior paint job can last five to ten years, though even mild wear and tear can make a good interior look old. I typically paint the entire interior of all my rehabs, regardless of the age of the home or the last time it was painted.

19

Scope of Work (SOW) Tasks

I typically paint the entire interior of every rehab I do, and rarely find the opportunity to either not paint or to just touch-up the existing paint. While there may be situations where you don't want to paint to save money, I highly recommend reconsidering, as a new paint job can make a tremendous difference in the aesthetics of your property.

PAINT INTERIOR	This includes walls, ceiling, and trim using a three-color paint scheme. I will do this in nearly 100 percent of my rehabs.

Cost Guidelines

With painting, you have the choice of getting either labor-only or labor-and-materials bids. Because good painters can generally get better discounts on materials than I can, and because buying and hauling around a lot of paint isn't fun, I much prefer to get combined labor-and-materials bids on jobs. My costs listed below will reflect both labor and material, though you are welcome to break out your costs based on the material cost information I provided earlier in this section.

Here are the cost guidelines associated with the interior painting tasks above:

PAINT INTERIOR	**$1.50-$2.25 per square foot of interior floor space.**
	Add 25 percent-35 percent if you're painting new sheetrock, going from light-to-dark or dark-to-light colors or if the walls are in bad shape.
	For my typical 2-story, 1,800-square-foot traditional houses, I generally pay about $3,000 for minor prep and painting of walls, ceiling, and trim.

Determining Your Local Prices

While you can ask a painter what their typical prices are, you'll rarely get an answer that is meaningful in terms of general pricing. My recommendation is to find a typical house that you'll be rehabbing, get several bids from different painters, and then use those bids to determine an approximate price per square foot for the painting. While a lot of painters will say they don't price per square foot of floor space (and they really don't think they do), their prices will tend to be pretty consistent on a square footage basis.

How to Pay for the Job

I like to pay for the painting at the completion of the work but will make some exceptions. If a painter is doing both the interior and exterior of the house, I will gladly pay for either the interior or the exterior when that part of the job is complete and then pay for the other half when that part of the job is complete.

On some occasions, a painter will ask for a deposit or for payment of materials upfront. If I have worked with the painter in the past, I may consider paying 20 percent upfront (which should cover material costs), or better yet, I may consider paying the paint supplier directly for the actual paint purchased.

Never pay more than 20 percent upfront for painting, as this will generally exceed the cost of materials necessary for the job.

COMPONENT #20
CABINETS AND COUNTERTOPS

Overview

They say kitchens and bathrooms sell houses and given that cabinetry and countertops are the centerpiece of kitchens and bathrooms, it's safe to say that cabinetry and countertops sell houses. While you probably don't need high-end custom cabinets to get your house sold (unless you're selling high-end custom houses, of course), choosing a good-looking but cost-efficient cabinet will help your property stand out without breaking the budget.

Here are some basics you should understand when choosing cabinets for your rehabs:

STOCK, SEMI-STOCK, AND CUSTOM

These are the three levels of cabinetry.

Stock cabinets are the most cost-efficient and can generally be bought off the shelf from big-box stores and cabinet suppliers. The big downside to stock cabinets is that you'll have a limited choice of color, wood, and style.

Semi-stock cabinets are a step up. They generally have a week or two lead time, but offer more variety in color and wood choices, as well as upgrades like pull-out shelves and quiet-close drawers.

Custom cabinets are the most expensive, as they are hand-built to your kitchen's specifications, including non-standard spaces and non-standard sizes.

FRAMED OR FRAMELESS

Framed cabinets are what you see in most houses. They consist of a cabinet box plus hinged doors that attach to the frame. Frameless cabinets have no "box," but instead have thick side panels for stability; the doors attach directly to the side panels.

PARTICLEBOARD, MDF, AND PLYWOOD

These are the three most common types of construction material used in cabinetry.

Particleboard is the lowest-quality material, made of wood shavings compressed into sheets. It is typically used in stock cabinets.

Medium-density fiberboard (MDF) is an engineered wood, is very dense, and is generally used in mid-range cabinetry.

Plywood is most commonly used in higher-end and custom cabinetry, as it is stronger and less prone to warping than the other materials.

LAMINATE AND WOOD VENEER

On top of the base cabinet construction material is an exterior material that gives the cabinet its look and feel. Laminates are the "plastic-y" feeling coatings used in lower-end cabinets; these coatings often peel or chip and are difficult to repair. Wood veneers are common, with typical wood species including oak, cherry, and maple in a variety of colors.

For typical low- to medium-end rehabs, I will typically use a framed, semi-stock cabinet made of MDF with a wood veneer. These are often available through local cabinet suppliers or special order through big-box stores and provide a great tradeoff in terms of affordability and visual appeal. Additionally, most semi-stock cabinets can be matched to bathroom vanities, which will ensure that your kitchen and bathrooms have a nice flow and common appearance.

For countertops, you have several choices, with the most common being laminate and granite.

LAMINATE

Laminate is probably the most cost-effective countertop material. Made of particleboard with layers of bonded plastic adhered to the top, you can find laminate in hundreds of colors and styles, including both matte and gloss finishes. While laminate is inexpensive, it isn't nearly as durable as higher-end countertops and is prone to scratching and burning.

GRANITE

Granite is the most common higher-end countertop material and is made of real stone—namely, granite. It comes in a range of colors, is scratch and heat resistant, and can give a kitchen a big "wow" factor. That said, granite is a good bit more expensive than laminate, and generally takes much longer to fabricate and install.

Personally, for my low-end rehabs, I use laminate countertops with a specific color and high-gloss finish that makes it look like granite. This is appealing to my lower-end buyers, but don't be fooled—the countertops may begin to show signs of wear within a few years. For my mid-level rehabs and above, I use granite. This adds quite a bit to the price, and also adds to the schedule, but in my area, it's a must-have in any property over $200,000. For my lower-end rehabs where I just want a bit of an advantage over the competition, I'll upgrade to granite countertops in the kitchen but use laminate countertops for the bathroom vanities. This saves some money but still gives a nice "wow" factor in the kitchen.

There are several other mid-grade countertop materials, including solid surface countertops and Corian countertops; but in my opinion, if you're going to use either of these, it's worth a little bit extra for the granite.

Which type of cabinets and countertops you use will be highly dependent on your area and your competition. I recommend that you don't try to skimp when it comes to cabinets and countertops, as they will make a big difference when trying to sell your house.

Inspection Tips

When inspecting cabinets and countertops, you should simply be considering the aesthetics and the functionality. In terms of aesthetics, you need to determine if the existing cabinets match the look and feel of the renovation. Is the style consistent with the rest of the finishes? Is the color appealing? Are the cabinets damaged or degrading?

Likewise with countertops—does the countertop material complement the rest of the finishes in the kitchen and the house? If you use mid- to high-end finishes in the rest of the house, you probably don't want to keep the laminate countertops in the kitchen or bathrooms.

In terms of functionality, you should operate every door and drawer to ensure they are hinged correctly and there are no major problems that would be difficult to correct or repair.

Life Expectancy

The life expectancy of cabinets and countertops is as follows:
- Cabinets: 15-25 years.
- Countertops:
  - Laminate: 10-15 years.
  - Granite: 25+ years.

Scope of Work (SOW) Tasks

Here are the SOW tasks associated with cabinets and countertops:

INSTALL KITCHEN CABINETS	I highly recommend finding a local cabinet supplier who is accustomed to working with investors. Most suppliers have access to low-end semi-stock cabinet lines that are perfect for lower-end rehab houses—they look and feel high-end but are still inexpensive.
	For kitchen cabinet installation, you can either have a professional cabinet installer (usually associated with the cabinet supplier) do the work, or you can have your carpenter do the installing. A professional installer will usually be more cost-effective and will generally be able to complete the job much more quickly. The benefit of using your carpenter is that if the installation is complicated, and any other kitchen changes need to be made to accommodate the cabinets, your carpenter can do those as well.
INSTALL BATHROOM VANITIES	I typically have my kitchen cabinet supplier provide matching bathroom vanities and allow the installer to install those. If for some reason I can't get matching vanities, the big box stores generally have decent all-in-one vanities for a very reasonable price that can be installed by our carpenter or handyman.
INSTALL COUNTERTOPS	When I use laminate tops, I will typically have my cabinet supplier order and install the tops along with the cabinets—he has the ability to get the laminate tops at a standard price. But for granite tops, I'll shop around, as you can typically find a granite supplier who is accustomed to working with investors who can beat most retail prices by quite a bit. For granite countertops, measuring and fabrication will need to be done after the cabinets are installed, and fabrication and installation will generally take one to two weeks. So, expect granite installation to add to your schedule a bit. Also, expect the granite supplier to provide and mount the undermount sinks as part of the installation.

Cost Guidelines

Here is what you should expect to pay for cabinet and countertop tasks:

INSTALL KITCHEN CABINETS	**Labor: $40-$60 per linear foot.** **Materials: $100-$250 per linear foot.** The linear foot measurement presumes a mix of both upper and lower cabinets, as well as room for appliances (fridge, range, dishwasher). If you're only buying base cabinets or wall cabinets, and not both, the price will tend towards the low end of this range. If you're using both base and wall cabinets for the entire linear footage, the price will tend towards the upper end of this range. The lower end of the material price is typical for the stock cabinets from the big-box stores, while the higher-end price is for nicer semi-stock stock cabinets. I typically pay right in the middle at about $150 per linear foot for decent semi-stock cabinets.
INSTALL BATHROOM VANITIES	**Labor: $75-$100 per vanity.** **Materials: $100-$400 per vanity.** Prices are based on typical cabinetry available at big-box stores and discount furniture and will range based on the type of cabinet (semi-custom or off-the-shelf) and size of cabinet (24"-60" are standard).
INSTALL COUNTERTOPS	**Laminate: $18-$25 per linear foot.** **Granite: $35-$50 per square foot.** As you can see, the range of granite prices is much larger than the range for laminate. This is because the price of granite depends on how common the coloring is. Other colors are less common, and therefore more expensive. The granite cost will often include all the holes cut out, plus undermount sinks, though some suppliers will charge extra for these—anywhere from $65 to $150 for cut-outs and sinks.

Determining Your Local Prices

It's easy to walk into your local big-box store and see what the prices are for their pre-assembled stock cabinets. For semi-stock cabinetry, start calling around to various cabinet suppliers in your city and ask if they have a line of semi-stock cabinetry they would recommend for a residential renovation. Cabinets are one area where having a good network of investors can be very helpful. In my experience, successful investors tend to know one or two cabinet suppliers who would otherwise be difficult to find.

As for granite prices, you'll need to decide what colors you prefer, and once you have some colors in mind you can start calling around to different granite suppliers in your area. This is another area where most successful investors will have a go-to professional who provides great pricing.

How to Pay for the Job

If you purchase from a big-box store, you'll pay for the cabinets when you purchase and then pay for installation after they are installed. If you purchase through a supplier who will be doing the installation, you may be required to pay upfront for the cabinets at the time they are ordered, and then pay for installation when the installer completes the job. If you have a good relationship with your cabinet supplier, you can generally negotiate to pay when the cabinets are delivered, as that's when the supplier normally pays for them.

COMPONENT #21
FLOORING

Overview

Most renovations are going to require at least some flooring replacement, and many will require all flooring to be installed or replaced. Because of this, flooring can end up being one of your largest renovation expenses.

There are many different flooring choices, and what you choose will be a product of where the house is, the competition, the level of rehab, and several other factors. Here are the most popular flooring choices for typical low- to mid-end rehabs:

- **Vinyl and linoleum:** A good low-end choice for kitchens and bathrooms, vinyl flooring comes in either large rolls (up to 12' long) that is installed similar to carpeting or comes in individual squares (generally 12" on a side) that are affixed individually by hand. Vinyl comes in many different "looks," with some vinyl replicating a hardwood look, some replicating a tile look, and some using very taste-specific designs and patterns.

- **Carpet:** This is the most common flooring type these days and is often used for bedrooms and hallways between bedrooms. In lower-end houses, you will often see carpeting in common living areas (living room, dining room), and in many of these types of houses, carpeting will be used in all areas other than the kitchen and bathrooms. When using carpeting, you will generally use an underlayment (padding) that will improve the feel of the carpet.

- **Laminate wood:** This is the low-end of "hardwood flooring," though to be precise, the flooring is made of a composite wood material and isn't pure wood. It is made of several layers of material, with the top layer being a protective coating, the second layer being a print layer that contains the visual look of the flooring, and the bottom layers comprising the structure of the flooring. Laminate flooring looks like hardwood and is scratch and stain resistant, making it a popular choice for lower-end renovations where real hardwood might not be economical.

- **Engineered hardwood:** Engineered wood flooring is made up of three to five layers of wood, with the bottom layers composed of cheaper hardwoods or plastics and the top layer being the actual flooring material (any type of hardwood, including oak, cherry, or bamboo) desired.

Engineered hardwoods are cheaper than solid hardwood because only the top veneer layer is the actual wood flooring. This type of flooring is also more moisture resistant than solid wood (you can't install solid wood below grade, but you can install engineered wood) and is also less likely to dry out, shrink, or warp.

The downside of engineered wood is that because only the top layer of the planks is actual hardwood flooring, you can only refinish the floors once or twice before you sand away the entire top veneer. Engineered wood is "pre-finished," which means that once the wood is installed, there is no additional work involved.

- **Solid hardwood:** This type of hardwood is one common wood species from top to bottom. Solid wood flooring can come in a large variety of wood species, including oak, birch, pine, cherry, bamboo, and beech. Because the entire plank is solid wood, it is generally more expensive than laminate or engineered flooring, but that also means that the wood can be refinished many times without any deterioration in the overall floor quality.

  Solid hardwoods come in two basic finishes—either pre-finished at the factory prior to installation or finished onsite. Finishing onsite tends to result in a nicer finish, but also requires onsite sanding, staining, and sealing, which is time consuming (several days from start to finish), messy, and more expensive.

  Note that all the hardwood flooring types come in several installation forms—floating (where the flooring planks are interlocked above the subfloor, but not attached directly to the subfloor), nail or staple down, or glue down. The type of installation will depend on the type of hardwood flooring used, the type of subfloor, and the preference of the investor.

- **Tile flooring:** Tile flooring comes in two common types—ceramic tile (made from fired clay) or natural stone (granite, marble, slate) There are many different varieties of ceramic and stone tile, and I can't even begin to get into the details here.

  In general, tile flooring is tremendously durable. But you'll pay for that durability—tile floors are expensive to install, and depending on the tile you purchase, may be expensive in terms of material as well.

A particular property will require more than one of these flooring choices, and you'll want to ensure that the group of flooring choices you use makes sense together, and the transitions between flooring in one area and another area aren't awkward.

For example, you'll rarely see vinyl flooring in one room that transitions into tile flooring in another. Likewise, you'll rarely ever use laminate, pre-finished, and site-finished hardwood in the same property, as these different flooring types resemble one another, but there is enough difference between them that it would look weird to use them together.

Lastly, before putting down any flooring material, you'll want to ensure that the subfloor (the material under the flooring—usually plywood) is in good condition, is uniform in height, and covers the entire area of the floor. Good flooring contractors can generally make minor subfloor repairs at the time of the flooring installation, but any major subfloor repair or replacement should be done by your carpenter before any finish flooring is installed.

Inspection Tips
The bulk of your flooring inspection will consist of visually determining whether the floors in your property are in sufficient condition to keep or need replacement.

That said, there are some additional situations you will occasionally encounter that you should be aware of:

- In houses built before the 1970s, it's always a good idea to check under carpet to determine if there is original hardwood that can be salvaged and refinished. Some of the nicest floors we've had in our rehabbed houses were original but hidden under old carpet or vinyl.
- If your house has a strong urine smell, and you suspect it's in the carpet, pad, or other flooring, consider that not only might you need to replace the flooring, but you might need to replace the subfloor as well. Pet urine will eventually soak through the top layer of flooring and into the subfloor. While an oil-based paint primer on the subfloor may be able to mask the smell, you should consider that there's a risk that this won't be enough, and the subfloor may need to be removed and replaced as well. Factor that into your budget.
- Finally, when inspecting floors, take a couple minutes to examine some of the higher-level concerns. For example, note whether any floors are sloped or highly out of level. For hardwoods, ensure that the planks aren't buckled (a common result of water damage) and that there aren't any major gaps between boards. Verify that there isn't any excessive

creaking on steps or "soft" areas that can be indicative of subfloor damage or a foundation issue.

Life Expectancy

Each flooring type has its own life expectancy:

- **Vinyl and linoleum:** If not ripped or torn, vinyl flooring can last 20 years or more. The biggest risk you face with vinyl is that styles tend to be very taste-specific, and the look of a particular vinyl flooring is more likely to change than the flooring is to deteriorate.
- **Carpet:** Professional carpet cleaning companies can help carpet to last 10+ years.
- **Laminate wood:** Laminate flooring is very hard and scratch resistant, but these floors can't be refinished, so if there are any stains, deep scratches, or other severe damage, the floor will need to be replaced. For this reason, expect laminate floors to last five to ten years under normal wear and tear, with high-quality laminate standing up the best.
- **Engineered hardwood:** Engineered wood can generally survive one or two refinishes, which should translate to 20 to 30 years if the floors are treated well and don't experience any abnormal wear and tear.
- **Solid hardwood:** Solid hardwood can be refinished many times, and therefore can last many decades. It is not uncommon to find houses built in the early 20th century with original hardwoods that can be refinished and look brand new.
- **Tile:** Tile floors are tremendously durable, and some can last hundreds of years. Natural stone tile is nearly as durable as concrete; and while ceramic tile will last a long time, it is susceptible to cracking if you drop something heavy on it.

Scope of Work (SOW) Tasks

There are lots of different tasks associated with installing, maintaining, and finishing floors. The most common tasks are addressed below:

21

REPLACE SUBFLOOR

Subfloor is typically made of either OSB (a cheaper version of plywood made of pressed wood flakes) or plywood and is between ¼" and ¾" in thickness. A carpenter or good handyman should be able to handle most subfloor repair and replacement tasks. Materials will include the plywood or OSB, as well as the fastening devices such as nails, screws, or adhesive.

I will generally allow the installer to provide all materials as part of their bid.

INSTALL VINYL OR LINOLEUM FLOORS

Rolled vinyl material and installation is generally measured in square yards as opposed to square feet (1 square yard = 9 square feet). Vinyl squares are generally measured per square foot (and each square is generally about one square foot in size, give or take). In addition to the actual vinyl material, an adhesive is used to attach the vinyl to the subfloor.

Many carpet installers will install vinyl flooring, though you may have to shop around to find someone who has a decent amount of experience and reasonable pricing.

I will generally provide the flooring material and have the installer provide the adhesive and other installation materials as part of their standard pricing.

INSTALL CARPET AND PAD

Carpet and pad material and installation is generally measured in square yards as opposed to square feet (1 square yard = 9 square feet). Carpet comes in many different varieties and pad comes in many different densities (weight). The most common pad weight is 6-pound pad, with 8-pound pad being a standard upgrade. Higher-density padding can make lower-end carpet feel like upgraded carpet, and pad is considerably cheaper than carpet; choosing a nice pad can improve the feel of your low-end carpet considerably.

You will want a contractor who specializes in carpet installation. Many contractors will say they can install carpet, but the installation quality tends to be noticeably lower when done by a non-specialist.

I will provide the carpet and pad myself and allow the installer to provide the tack strips and other installation materials as part of their standard pricing.

CLEAN CARPET	Carpet cleaning can be a DIY job, but it's more trouble than what most investors will want to try to do themselves. A good carpet cleaning company can get out most typical stains and can make old carpet appear new. Carpet cleaners generally charge per room (not square foot or square yard), and the more rooms you have done at once, the bigger the discount.
INSTALL LAMINATE WOOD	Wood flooring installation is measured in square feet. The big decision you'll need to make with laminate flooring is how it will be installed: floating, glue down, or nail down. Floating tends to be the most common installation method for laminate floors, making laminate a good choice for older houses that have particle board subfloor that can't be used with nail-down or glue-down floors (particle board subfloor was common in houses built during the 1970s). I generally use a hardwood installer or carpenter to install laminate flooring. A good handyman can generally handle the job, assuming he is precise with his cuts and is detail-oriented. I will generally provide the laminate flooring and allow the installer to provide the underlayment and any other installation materials as part of their standard pricing.
INSTALL ENGINEERED HARDWOOD	Wood flooring installation is measured in square feet. The two big decisions you'll need to make with engineered wood flooring is what kind of wood you'll use and how it will be installed: floating, glue down, or nail down. Floating and nail down tend to be the most common installation method for engineered wood floors, but glue-down floors are fairly common as well. I will generally provide the engineered wood flooring and allow the installer to provide the underlayment and any other installation materials as part of their standard pricing.

21

21

INSTALL SOLID HARDWOOD (PRE-FINISHED)	Wood flooring installation is measured in square feet. Almost all solid hardwood is nail down, so the big decision you'll need to make when purchasing pre-finished flooring is the species of wood. For solid hardwood floors, I highly recommend using a qualified hardwood installer. I will generally allow the installer to provide all flooring and installation materials as part of their bid. I will have the installer provide samples prior to purchase of the materials and installation so I know exactly what I'm getting.
INSTALL SOLID HARDWOOD (SITE FINISHED)	Wood flooring installation is measured in square feet. Almost all solid hardwood is nail down, and most site-finished hardwood is oak. You'll need to choose a stain color that the installer will use when staining the floor. After installation, the finisher will sand the floors and apply a coat of stain. Once that stain dries (about 24 hours), another light sanding will be done, and a polyurethane sealant will be applied, which will take another 24 hours or so to dry. For site-finished solid hardwood floors, I highly recommend using a qualified hardwood installer. I will always allow the installer to provide the wood and the installation materials as part of their bid.
REFINISH HARDWOOD	Hardwood refinishing is measured in square feet. Refinishing involves sanding the existing hardwood floors to remove the existing polyurethane topcoat or stain, expose the natural wood grain, staining, and then sealing the floors. Just like the site-finishing discussed above, the process will be done in two steps over several days.
INSTALL TILE	Tile installation is measured in square feet. For simple jobs, a qualified handyman can generally handle the task. But for any tile work that is intricate or requires lots of detail, I highly recommend using a contractor who specializes in tile installation. I will provide the tile and the grout and allow the contractor to provide the rest of the installation materials as part of their standard pricing or bid.

Cost Guidelines

The following is a general overview of the costs for each of the flooring tasks outlined above:

REPLACE SUBFLOOR	Labor: $.60-$.85 per square foot.
	Materials: $.75-$1.00 per square foot.
	Material prices will primarily be determined by type of subfloor material to be used. OSB is generally a satisfactory subfloor choice (lower end of the price range), though in some cases, you may prefer plywood instead (higher end of the price range). Your contractor will also need nails or screws, and perhaps some adhesive as part of the materials purchase. Labor will vary greatly based on the type of contractor who does the work. A skilled carpenter will cost more than a handyman but will do a better job. For all flooring jobs, to account for waste I would recommend budgeting for 10 percent more material than actually measured.
INSTALL VINYL OR LINOLEUM	ROLLED:
	Labor: $4-$6 per square yard for rolled.
	Materials: $8-$12 per square yard for rolled.
	SQUARES:
	Labor: $1.00-$1.50 per square foot for squares.
	Materials: $1-$2 per square foot for squares.
	For all flooring jobs, to account for waste I would recommend budgeting for 10 percent more material than actually measured.
INSTALL CARPET AND PAD	Labor: $4-$7 per square yard.
	Materials: $10-$18 per square yard for carpet.
	$2-$3 per square yard for pad.
	For all flooring jobs, to account for waste I would recommend budgeting for 10 percent more material than actually measured.

CLEAN CARPET	**$50-$80 per room.**
INSTALL LAMINATE WOOD	**Labor: $1.50-$3.50 per square foot.** **Materials: $.50-$3.50 per square foot.** For all flooring jobs, to account for waste I would recommend budgeting for 10 percent more material than actually measured.
INSTALL ENGINEERED HARDWOOD	**Labor: $1.50-$3.50 per square foot.** **Materials: $1-$5 per square foot.** For all flooring jobs, to account for waste I would recommend budgeting for 10 percent more material than actually measured.
INSTALL SOLID HARDWOOD (PRE-FINISHED)	**Labor: $1.50-$3.50 per square foot.** **Materials: $2-$5 per square foot.** For all flooring jobs, to account for waste I would recommend budgeting for 10 percent more material than actually measured.
INSTALL SOLID HARDWOOD (SITE FINISHED)	**Labor: $3-$4 per square foot.** **Materials: $1.50-$4.50 per square foot.** Oak flooring is the most common type of site-finished solid hardwood flooring, and costs are relatively uniform. Higher grade oak (referred to as No. 1 wood) is generally a bit more expensive, as are wider planks. Higher grade wood contains fewer knots and is more uniform in appearance, and should be used when using light-colored stains, as the natural wood appearance will be more readily visible. Other wood varieties are also available unfinished, with prices both less than and more than oak flooring, depending on your preference. For all flooring jobs, to account for waste I would recommend budgeting for 10 percent more material than actually measured.

REFINISH HARDWOOD	$1.50-$2.00 per square foot.
	There may be an extra cost if the existing wood is in very bad condition and requires patching or repairs prior to refinishing.
INSTALL TILE	Labor: $3-$6 per square foot.
	Materials: $1-$10 per square foot.
	For all flooring jobs, to account for waste I would recommend budgeting for 10 percent more material than actually measured.

Determining Your Local Prices

Most flooring contractors can tell you their labor prices for typical floor-ing installation over the phone. In cases where the contractor will be providing the flooring material as well as the installation, make sure you get a break down of the labor cost versus the material cost, just to make sure both costs are in line with your expectations. In fact, don't hesitate to ask the contractor directly if he'll be making a profit on the materials, and let him know that you expect materials to be provided at cost or you'll provide your own materials for the job. You shouldn't have to pay mark-up on flooring materials unless the marked-up price is still cheaper than what you can get yourself, which is unlikely.

How to Pay for the Job

If you provide the materials, all payments should be made at the end of the completed job. If the contractor provides the materials, it is standard that you pay for the materials upfront.

COMPONENT #22
PERMITS

Overview

A common question new investors have is, "When do I need permits?" This is a tough question to answer and will be based on the requirements in your local jurisdiction and the scope of your project. Obviously, not having to get permits makes a renovation cheaper and easier but having the inspections that go along with permitting can provide a level of confidence to your buyer that everything was done safely and up to code. More importantly, if you don't get permits when required, this can make selling the property very difficult, as many lenders will ask for proof of inspections prior to providing funding for your buyer.

There are basically two kinds of permits: specialty permits and building permits.

Specialty permits are for things like electrical, plumbing, HVAC, foundation, or roofing, and can generally be pulled by the specialty contractor himself, assuming he has the proper licensing credentials and insurance.

Building permits are for larger jobs, where you will be doing many of these tasks—for example, when doing an addition, doing structural work, or finishing an area. Building permits either need to be pulled by the homeowner or a licensed general contractor. In my area, a homeowner can only pull building permits if the house is his primary residence, so I can't pull permits on my investment properties, only my GC can. That means I need to hire a licensed GC every time I do a large renovation job.

If you do need building permits, there are generally three steps involved:

1. Create drawings
2. File for permits
3. Inspections

CREATE DRAWINGS

While this step won't always be required, if you'll be doing an addition, finishing a space, or moving walls, the building department will likely require you to submit architectural drawings along with your permit application. This is so the building inspector can determine if what you're doing is permissible and then also to ensure that your contractors do what you have stated you're going to do.

Drawings are generally done by architects, but some GCs have the ability to do basic drawings required by some jurisdictions. I've even had one case where the inspector allowed me to do a freehand drawing on a piece of paper to indicate a small renovation job I was completing. If you're going to need drawings, ask your GC for an architect recommendation, or talk to other investors who may know a reasonably priced architect.

To determine whether you need drawings for your project, I recommend calling the building department directly and speaking with one of the inspectors. Regardless of whether drawings are needed for permits, they're always nice to have for your contractors, as they should indicate everything you plan to do on the renovation, thus eliminating a lot of confusion if your contractors have questions.

FILE FOR PERMITS

Once your drawings are complete (assuming you need them), you'll fill out a form at your building department that will overview the work you plan to do and provide names, phone numbers, and license numbers for your contractors. You will pay a fee either at the time you file for the permits or when they are granted, which could take anywhere from a few minutes to a few weeks, depending on the scope of the work and your jurisdiction.

A building inspector may come to the property to see the current condition and will ultimately determine if your plans are reasonable and up to current building codes. A building inspector may sometimes require that you provide engineering reports if you'll be doing structural work and may call you or your GC to ask questions and get more information. In some cases, the inspector may require a survey of the property, especially when building an addition, constructing a deck, or doing other exterior modifications.

INSPECTIONS

Once your permits have been granted, you're free to begin work, but you'll be required to have inspections by the building inspector at various checkpoints throughout the project. During these inspections, the building inspector will check to make sure things were done properly and up to code, and if he finds something wrong, you'll have to fix it and order a new inspection before you can move on to the next checkpoint.

One thing to keep in mind is that building inspectors can look at anything they want when they're in your house. If an inspector is doing an electrical inspection and notices that a plumbing component is not up to code, he can make you fix it. Any time you get permits and have building inspections, be prepared to ensure that every part of the house is up to code and will pass inspection, even if it wasn't something you were planning on renovating. This is why rehabbers often don't like to open up walls if they don't have to—once the wall is open, if the inspector finds a problem, you'll need to fix it.

It's also important to note that in many jurisdictions, in order to pull permits you need to have a general contractor's license, even if you own the house. That means if you're going to be doing work that requires permits, you might need to hire a GC to run your project. In fact, even if you're not going to be pulling permits, you might decide that going the GC route is the right decision.

Inspection Tips
N/A

Life Expectancy
N/A

Scope of Work (SOW) Tasks
Here are the common tasks associated with getting permits:

PERMIT DRAWINGS	As mentioned above, when required, you'll need drawings to accompany your permit application.
PERMITS	As mentioned above, when required, you'll need to file a permit application and be granted permits before you can start on your job.
INSPECTIONS	As mentioned above, you'll be required to go through inspection checkpoints throughout your renovation.

GENERAL CONTRACTOR FEES	General contractors will charge either a flat fee for their services or a percentage of the total renovation cost. It's up to you and your GC to negotiate the details and come to an agreement on how you want the relationship to work.

Cost Guidelines

22

Here is how I budget for permitting tasks:

PERMIT DRAWINGS	**$40-$70 per hour.** My architect generally charges $45 per hour for permit drawings, and he will file for the permits as well. For a typical single-level drawing (reconfiguring one floor of the house or finishing a basement, for example), complete with cross sections and 3D renderings, I will generally pay $800 to $1,000. For more complex drawings, or for new house plans, expect prices up to $3,000 or more.
PERMITS	**$35-$2,000.** The exact amount of the permits will be based upon specific jurisdiction and the scope of the work being performed. Every local permitting authority will have their own permitting process and fees associated with the process. In my jurisdiction, there is a $100 fee to review the permit application and then the permit/inspection fees are based on the square footage of the property and the types of permits requested. In general, I'll pay $200 to $400 for permits on a typical renovation that includes finishing or reconfiguring a large space.

INSPECTIONS	**$50-$100 per inspection.** The building inspector will not generally charge for inspections, but my GC will generally charge between $20 and $25 per hour to have one of his qualified contractors attend an inspection. Because building inspectors generally provide only a time window, the contractor could be sitting for several hours before the inspector shows up, and I'll be paying for that time. But it's still more cost efficient than having to be there myself.
GENERAL CONTRACTOR FEES	**7 percent-15 percent of renovation costs.** Most GCs will charge a percentage of the renovation costs to run the project from beginning to end. This includes supplying the contractors, materials, and expertise to complete the job on schedule and on budget. If you only need a GC to pull permits for you, some GCs will be willing to do this for between $200 and $1,000, depending on your relationship with them and the scope of the job.

Determining Your Local Prices

For architectural drawings, an architect should be able to tell you over the phone how he charges—whether per project or per hour—and give you a ballpark figure of what it would cost to do drawings for a particular area of the house.

For permit costs, visit your local building department or permit office. They'll provide you with a list of fees associated with filing for and getting permits.

If you plan to work with a GC, I highly recommend talking to other investors in your area and finding a GC who is accustomed to working with investors. Once you have a relationship with the GC and each understands what is needed, you should then discuss pricing.

How to Pay for the Job

Most architects will require a retainer or down payment upfront, with the rest of the payment due upon providing the final drawings. Your permit office will determine how permits are paid for.

COMPONENT #23
MOLD

Overview

For many investors, mold is the most terrifying renovation issue they'll ever face. Hopefully, after reading this section, that won't be the case anymore.

Mold is a fungus that occurs naturally in the environment, mostly in soil and on dead or decaying organisms. In fact, if you were to do a mold test outdoors, you'd find that the mold spore count is pretty high. But you don't generally worry about encountering mold outside, do you?

Mold only becomes a problem when it starts to grow in exceptionally large quantities indoors, or when certain types of dangerous mold spores start to grow. In order to grow, mold needs two things: moisture and a food source such as wood, insulation, sheetrock, or cloth. If you take away either the moisture source or the food source, mold will stop growing.

When you have mold growing in a house, the remediation course involves three steps:

1. Remediate the moisture source.
2. Remove the mold that has grown.
3. Perform mold test to verify remediation.

Common moisture sources are leaks (for example, in a roof, a water heater, a toilet) or high humidity from a house being unoccupied and closed up for a long time. Once the moisture source is removed—the leak fixed or the humidity problem resolved—the mold will stop growing. At that point, once the existing mold is removed—for example, by removing any moldy sheetrock, flooring, or cabinets—the problem is resolved.

An air quality test (AQT) can tell you the count and type of mold spores in the air, so you'll know if the problem has been adequately resolved; and once you confirm the mold has gone through a third-party mold test, you can put the house back together.

Only an AQT can tell you for certain if your house has mold and what type of mold, but if you see mold in a house, that's a pretty reliable indicator. Some people believe that if you smell mold, there is a big problem. In reality, many distressed houses haven't been lived in for long periods of time, and it's pretty common for these closed up houses to smell musty without there being a major mold issue. In many cases, opening up the windows for a couple days or getting the air conditioning running again with take care of the smell, and an AQT will indicate that there are no remaining mold issues.

That said, if there is a mold problem, the first course of action is going to be to determine the source of moisture and get it remediated. This should be done prior to bringing in a mold remediator, as remediating the mold won't be a long-term fix if the moisture problem isn't resolved—the mold will just grow back.

At any time in the process, you have the option to bring in a testing company. But if you're fairly certain that there is a mold problem, the testing will only confirm what you already know. Save your money, do the remediation, and then do the testing at the end to confirm that the remediation worked.

Regardless of what anyone tells you, mold remediation of any area larger than ten square feet is not a DIY project. Instead, you'll want to bring in a qualified mold remediator. Different states have different requirements for licensing mold remediators—in some states, you need to be licensed to legally remediate mold problems; in other states, there are no requirements whatsoever, so finding a qualified remediator can be a bit more difficult.

Once the remediator evaluates the problem, it's very likely he'll recommend removing any porous building materials that have been impacted by the mold. This might include wet sheetrock, wet carpet and pad, and moldy cabinets. While you may be able to do this demo yourself, some areas have very strict biohazard rules around disposing of moldy material. Ask your mold remediator if you can do the demo yourself or if he recommends doing it himself.

I look at mold problems just like I look at roof issues, cracked windows, or dirty carpet—it's going to require bringing in a knowledgeable contractor or two, paying some money, and getting the work done. While it may be more expensive and time consuming than those other fixes, ultimately, it's no more complicated or daunting. I don't let mold stop me from buying a house at the appropriate price discount, and neither should you. Just note that, in some states, you will be required to disclose the mold to future buyers; if you had the work done by a reputable contractor, you should also have a warranty that will ease the buyer's minds and you'll hopefully find that resale isn't any more difficult than if the mold were never there.

Inspection Tips

There are several ways to do a cursory mold inspection in a property that you're walking through, but the most basic—and often the most accurate—is to simply use the sniff test. Mold tends to have a very distinctive smell, and after you've smelled it once, you're unlikely to forget it.

Keep in mind that a musty smell isn't always indicative of mold—houses that have been closed up for long periods of time without much airflow will often have a stale odor. It's common for foreclosed homes, or homes where the electricity is turned off, to have a strong smell of stale air and mustiness. If you come across this in the property you're inspecting, don't be alarmed—but definitely take note and do some additional investigation and due diligence to determine if mold is the issue or not.

In addition to smelling for mold, you should be on the lookout for mold on walls, in closets and especially in any place where there is a risk of water intrusion or leaks. When I inspect a property, I always carry a flashlight, and do a detailed search of all parts of the basement, attic, and garage—three places where mold is exceedingly common.

On any property where I find or suspect mold, I will open up some of the vents and ducts to investigate if there is mold growing in the HVAC system. This is a common health hazard that is often overlooked by investors, but for the couple hundred dollars that it costs to have HVAC ducts cleaned and disinfected, it doesn't need to be.

Finally, remember that mold can sometimes be very difficult to find, even if you smell it or otherwise suspect that it's there. If you suspect there is mold in a property, but can't verify it yourself, I highly recommend bringing in a specialist to investigate further.

Life Expectancy

N/A

Scope of Work (SOW) Tasks

Here are the major tasks associated with mold remediation:

REMEDIATE WATER SOURCE	This task actually isn't part of this section. Removing a moisture source should be done as part of whatever major component is causing the moisture. If it's a roof leak, you should resolve the problem when doing roof work. If it's a plumbing leak, you should resolve the problem as part of the plumbing renovations. If it's a foundation issue, you should be resolving the issue as part of your foundation work. Any moisture issue should be resolved *prior* to doing any mold testing or remediation.
DEMO MOLDY MATERIAL	This is another task that isn't really part of the mold remediation. Depending on the scope of the problem, you may need to do extra demo to remove moldy sheetrock, flooring, and cabinets. Depending on the rules in your state and the extent of the problem, you may need a more complex demo process to avoid any contamination from the moldy materials.
AIR QUALITY TEST (AQT)	To verify whether there is still a mold problem, or to find out the specific types of molds present, an air quality test can be performed. These tests should definitely be done after mold remediation to ensure the problem was adequately resolved. While air tests are the most common type of testing, in some cases the testing company may recommend a surface test, where a sample is taken from the floor or a framing member in order to verify that there is no mold on those surfaces.

23

There are many ways to remediate existing mold, depending on the scope of the problem, the location of the mold, and the type of mold. And if you ask five different mold remediators how to resolve a specific problem, you'll likely get five different answers.

In general, the process involves ensuring that the water source is remediated, killing existing mold using a biocide, removing existing spores through sanding or wire brushing, and then maybe encapsulating the previously contaminated areas using a sealant. Some remediators will use encapsulation to remediate hard to reach areas or to ensure that the dead mold spores do not get released into the air or affect the surrounding areas. Don't hire a mold remediator who plans to *only* encapsulate *instead of* killing and removing the mold—this is a substandard method that many scam remediators like to use. In many cases, the remediator will put dehumidifiers in the house for several days post-remediation; this will remove any humidity from the air and will dry out the house as a final remediation step.

There are lots of different techniques that can be used for killing, removing, and encapsulating mold; unfortunately, even if I were to spend the next 20 pages discussing the details of mold remediation (not that I know enough to fill that much space), I wouldn't be able to generalize what mold remediation techniques to use under what circumstances.

23

Cost Guidelines

There are so many different circumstances surrounding mold problems and so many different remediation techniques that it's nearly impossible to outline what the cost of a particular job should be without having all the details about the particular property and the exact problem. Here are some tips on what to expect when getting quotes for mold work:

AIR QUALITY TEST (AQT)	**$100-$200 per test.** This is pretty standard pricing for third-party air quality tests or surface tests. The variable that is hard to determine without specific knowledge of the problem is how many tests will be needed. If the mold is confined to a small location (a room or crawlspace, for example), a single test might be sufficient. If the mold was airborne and suspected to have contaminated the entire house, the testing company may recommend two air quality tests per floor, and perhaps one or two surface tests as well. In general, I like to budget $500 for testing when I'm dealing with a medium- or large-sized mold issue.
MOLD REMEDIATION	**$500-$10,000+.** While you may be able to remediate small problems for less than $500 and you could someday run into a problem that will cost more than $10,000 to fix completely, on a typical 2,000 square foot or smaller house, that range should cover pretty much every mold problem you'll encounter. To know exactly what a project will cost, you'll need to get several bids. Remember, mold remediators recognize that mold is a scary topic, and will often use this fact to hike up their prices, telling you that if you find a solution that costs anything less, you'll be endangering your family or whoever ultimately moves into the house. This may or may not be the truth, but in general, the cost of remediation will be relative to the amount of time it takes to remediate, and the amount of manual labor involved. Make sure you ask lots of questions about how the remediation will be done and how long it will take. If the remediator plans to put dehumidifiers into the house to complete the job, expect to pay $50-$100 per day for each dehumidifier. While this may be a necessary part of the remediation, this can significantly drive up the price of the job.

23

Determining Your Local Prices

The only way to know for certain what a mold remediation job will cost is to get several quotes from qualified contractors. Once you find a qualified contractor you like and trust, he may be able to give you some general guidelines that you can use for future pricing.

How to Pay for the Job

Most remediation companies will ask for the work to be paid in several draws that correspond to the specific work being done. For example, a company I often work with likes to get one-third of the price upfront (the morning work starts), one-third after the bulk of the remediation is completed, and then one-third after third-party testing has been completed and has verified the problem is resolved.

23

COMPONENT #24
TERMITES

Overview

Depending on which part of the country you invest in, termites may or may not be common problem. In Atlanta, where I typically do my rehabs, termites are a way of life. We like to talk about there being two types of houses: those that have termites and those that will get termites.

There are actually four different types of termites that are common in the United States:

SUBTERRANEAN TERMITES

These types of termites are found in every state in the U.S. except Alaska and are especially prevalent in warmer climates. They are extremely destructive because they work quickly and in large colonies. The colonies live in the soil around the house and build mud tubes by which they can travel to and from the wood inside the house. These types of termites will even eat through sheetrock and paper. In houses that have subterranean termites, you'll often see dirt trails on wood or concrete—this is how the termites travel.

DRYWOOD TERMITES

These types of termites are most prevalent in the southern states, as they can't survive in sub-freezing temperatures. Florida and Texas houses tend to be very susceptible to drywood termites. Evidence of these types of termites includes small, oval fecal droppings around damaged areas. Drywood termite colonies can often only be removed through fumigation of the house.

DAMPWOOD TERMITES

These are the least dangerous, least destructive, and least likely to invade your home. Because they need moisture to survive, they are most likely to be found on the exterior of the house, in wood piles, on wet siding, or around wet wood caused by plumbing leaks. Getting rid of dampwood termites is simple—just remove or fix the source of moisture that attracted the termites.

FORMOSAN TERMITES

These termites are a kind of subterranean termite and are extremely destructive. They live in warmer climates and are most commonly found in Alabama, Florida, California, Georgia, Hawaii, Louisiana, Mississippi, North Carolina, South Carolina, Tennessee, and Texas. Often referred to as "super termites," they are among the most voracious and aggressive of over 2,000 termite species known to science, and will chew through wood, flooring, and even wallpaper undetected.

While many people are scared of termite-ridden or termite-damaged houses, these types of properties can be a great opportunity for knowledgeable investors, as other investors are often scared away. When it comes to dealing with a termite issue, the process is actually quite simple:

1. Remediate any existing termite damage.
2. Get a reputable pest/termite company to treat and maintain a termite bond.

Of course, just because the process is simple doesn't mean it's necessarily inexpensive. Depending on how much damage has been done by existing termites, the repairs could be substantial, especially if the termites have damaged framing or compromised walls. Oftentimes, though, the damage is superficial, with just small, localized repairs needed. It's often difficult to determine the extent of termite damage without tearing out some sheetrock or siding and actually viewing the framing members of the house.

If you live in a place where termites are common, or if you suspect you have termites at your house, the first thing I recommend is to call a local pest control company that handles termite remediation to get an inspection. Many of these companies will perform a free inspection, and can tell you if you have termites, what kind, and the cost of treatment.

If you find that you have termites, you'll want to do some further inspection to determine if there is existing damage. Oftentimes a GC or carpenter can help assess termite damage and give you a bid to remediate.

Inspection Tips

Termite infestation and damage can be difficult to detect for those not trained to know what to look for. That said, there's a trick I use that has helped me to identify larger termite issues that I otherwise would have missed.

As I'm walking the interior and exterior of the house, I'll hold my house keys in my hand. I'll randomly poke the tip of the key into any wood trim or siding. If the wood is sound, the key will bounce off with a dull thud; but, if there is termite damage, the key will either leave an indentation or go directly through the wood.

Keep in mind that just because the key goes through the wood doesn't mean there are termites. In some cases, the wood could be rotted from water damage, mold, or fungus. But if you find any areas where the wood is soft or crumbly—especially on the interior of the property—you should have a professional take a closer look.

Life Expectancy
N/A

Scope of Work (SOW) Tasks
Here are the most common tasks associated with termite control and treatment:

TERMITE INSPECTION	Many pest control companies will do a free inspection. They expect that if they find a termite issue, you will pay for treatment, which is why they are willing to perform the inspection for free. They can tell you if you have termites, the type of termites, and may be able to help you identify the location and extent of existing damage.
TERMITE TREATMENT	If you have termites, you'll want to get the house treated so that no further damage will be done. Depending on the type of termite, the scope of the problem, and the company you choose, the treatment could include using bait traps (baits with paper or cardboard that go in the ground around the house containing a lethal substance that termites will take to their colonies), liquid treatments (holes are drilled around the foundation perimeter and toxic liquid poured in, creating a barrier that keeps termites out), or fumigation (sealing your home for several days and using toxic gas to kill the termites). There are several other treatment methods, but those are the most common.

TERMITE LETTER	Once your house has been inspected and treated, and the pest control company is satisfied that there is no termite issue with the property, they can supply a letter to this effect that you can provide to your buyer. Many buyers will require that you provide a clean termite letter prior to sale of the property, so even if you don't suspect you have a termite problem, getting an inspection and termite letter is a good idea.

Cost Guidelines

The cost guidelines below do not include remediation of existing damage. This work will be part of other major components—most likely as part of the framing or carpentry component:

24

TERMITE INSPECTION	Generally free
TERMITE TREATMENT	**$600-$1,200 for baiting ($4-$6 per linear foot).** **$600-$1,200 for chemical treatment ($4-$6 per linear foot).** **$1,000-$3,000 for fumigation ($1-$2 per square foot).** These prices assume a standard 1,500-2,000 square foot property. For larger properties, the cost could be considerably higher. With treatment will come a bond or warranty renewable on an annual basis. The renewal costs tend to range from $200-$350 per year.
TERMITE LETTER	**$35-$100.**

Determining Your Local Prices

I would recommend having several different pest control companies visit your property, inspect, and give you a recommendation on treatment. Even if they say you don't have termites, they'll be happy to give you a bid to do the work to ensure you don't get termites. Use this opportunity to ask what kind of treatment they would recommend and the cost. They may be willing to give you a price per square foot or per linear foot to help make future estimation easier.

How to Pay for the Job

Always pay for termite treatment work after the work is completed and you've been provided with a clean termite letter and warranty.

24

COMPONENT #25
MISCELLANEOUS

Overview

There is no specific list of "miscellaneous" items that need to be included in your rehab, but you'll find after a few projects that you start to have various work items that aren't included in any of the other major components I discuss in this book.

Here are some examples:

- Replacing doorknobs on interior doors and new deadbolts on exterior doors.
- Replacing door stops and hinge stops.
- Replacing register and return grates (if your HVAC company doesn't do it).
- Replacing glass shower doors.
- Installing cabinet undermount microwave ovens.
- Replacing switches, outlets, switch plates, and outlet covers.
- Installing mini-blinds.

In addition to these tasks are the punch list and inspection repairs. The punch list comprises the issues that you found during the final days of rehab that weren't done properly or were overlooked. Inspection repairs are those repairs requested by the buyer after he completes his inspections.

I like to factor in a miscellaneous budget on every project, and I often find that I use up most of that budget on the items above as well as random little things that come up throughout the project. Most of these tasks are completed by my handyman, whom I pay hourly.

The other cost I often factor into this section is the cost of appliances, if I will be providing them.

Inspection Tips

When considering the miscellaneous items that should be addressed during a renovation, I like to use the "trusted friend" approach. What this involves is having a friend—someone who represents a typical buyer for this type of house—walk into the house with a roll of blue painter tape and use the tape to mark everything he finds that draws his negative attention or that he finds to be a detractor in the finishes.

Perhaps he notices that a light switch cover is tilted in an annoying fashion, or a light figure doesn't match the theme of the finishes, or a paint streak is jumping off the wall. Maybe he opens a door and thinks, "This door should open in the opposite direction." Or maybe he points out that the toilet in the master bath is configured in a way that provides too little privacy.

These are the things that you and your contractors are just too close to the project to notice. But they are things that a potential buyer—who is just walking the house for the first time—will notice. And this is your opportunity to address these concerns before risking turning off any buyers.

Make it a rule that before you put any house on the market, you have two or three trusted friends walk the house and give you feedback.

Life Expectancy
N/A

Scope of Work (SOW) Tasks
Instead of breaking out the multitude of "miscellaneous" tasks individually, I like to create a separate line that covers all miscellaneous tasks:

MISCELLANEOUS TASKS	This line item is included in every project.
APPLIANCES	If you will be purchasing appliances that will stay with the property, you should include them here.
HOUSE CLEANING	I always have my house professionally cleaned after renovations are complete and prior to our first showing.

Cost Guidelines

Here is how I budget for miscellaneous tasks:

MISCELLANEOUS TASKS	$500-$2,000.
	I will generally budget $1,000 for miscellaneous tasks on any project that is more than just a "paint and carpet" rehab. For very small rehabs, I would still budget at least $500, and for large rehabs, budgeting up to $2,000 isn't a bad idea—you'd be surprised some of the little things that pop up during a big rehab.
	In my experience, about half of this budget will be spent on a good handyman, and the rest will be spent on random materials needed to complete the tasks. A good handyman will run $20 or $30 an hour, and as long as he's truly good at what he does, he'll be worth every penny.
APPLIANCES	The cost of appliances can vary widely, depending on the type and quality you purchase. Personally, I like to put low-end stainless appliances in every property and will sometimes include a washer/dryer set as well, especially for the lower-end properties where I know I'll have competition and where a washer/dryer can really make my property stand out.
	Here are standard prices for new, builder-grade appliances that can be purchased at the big-box stores or local appliance suppliers:
	Refrigerator: $500-$900.
	Range: $500-$700.
	Dishwasher: $300-$500.
	Microwave: $150-$250.
	Washer/dryer set: $800-$1,000.
	All installations should be straightforward with the exception of the dishwasher—which is covered in the plumbing section—and the microwave, which will likely need to be mounted above the range. A carpenter or handyman should be able to complete the installation of the microwave for between $50 and $100.

25

HOUSE CLEANING	**$150-$300.**
	Cost will depend on the size of the house and the scope of the work. Ironically, the larger the rehab, generally the less house cleaning is needed, as most of the finishes and surfaces are brand new. But there are always remaining dust, debris, and stickers on fixtures that need to be cleaned, and a sparkly house is always a better selling point than a dirty, dusty one.

Determining Your Local Prices

Finding a great handyman will increase your chances of success as an investor, and I would highly recommend you spend some time talking to other local investors and getting recommendations for a great handyman. Most handymen work on an hourly rate, so after explaining to them the types of tasks you're looking to have done, they should be able to tell you what they charge.

How to Pay for the Job

Most handymen will expect to get paid at the end of every day, after work is completed. If you have several days' worth of work, expect to write a check at the end of each day for the work accomplished that day. I will never pay a handyman upfront, unless it is for specific materials that he'll be purchasing for me.

SECTION 4
PUTTING IT ALL TOGETHER

The previous section detailed the SOW tasks and costs associated with each of our 25 major components. Below is all the information captured in a single table.

TASK	UNIT	LABOR	MATERIALS
ROOF			
ROOF MAINTENANCE	PER HOUSE	$250-$500	*
REPLACE SHEATHING	PER SHEET	$40-$50	*
ROOF REPLACEMENT			
ASPHALT SHINGLES	PER SQUARE	$180-$350	*
WOOD SHINGLES	PER SQUARE	$450-$700	*
STEEL ROOF	PER SQUARE	$350-$900	*
ALUMINUM ROOF	PER SQUARE	$750-$1,000	*
SLATE ROOF	PER SQUARE	$1,000-$3,000	*

TASK	UNIT	LABOR	MATERIALS
GUTTERS/SOFFIT/FASCIA			
CLEAN GUTTERS	PER HOUSE	$100-$300	*
REPLACE GUTTERS			
ALUMINUM GUTTER	PER LF	$4-$8	*
STEEL GUTTER	PER LF	$4-$8	*
VINYL/PLASTIC GUTTER	PER LF	$3-$5	*
COPPER/ZINC GUTTER	PER LF	$15-$30	*
REPLACE SOFFIT/FASCIA			
WOOD SOFFIT/FASCIA	PER LF	$5-$10	*
VINYL SOFFIT/FASCIA	PER LF	$6-$12	*
ALUMINUM SOFFIT/FASCIA	PER LF	$8-$15	*
SIDING			
PRESSURE WASH	PER HOUSE	$200-$500	*
REMOVE OLD SIDING	PER SQUARE	$50-$100	*
REPLACE SHEATHING	PER SHEET	$40-$50	*
REPLACE HOUSE WRAP	PER HOUSE	$300-$600	*
PATCH SIDING	PER SF	$3-$6	*
REPLACE SIDING			
WOOD SIDING	PER SQUARE	$400-$700	*
ALUMINUM SIDING	PER SQUARE	$200-$350	*

TASK	UNIT	LABOR	MATERIALS
VINYL SIDING	PER SQUARE	$150-$350	*
CEMENT BOARD SIDING	PER SQUARE	$300-$600	*
MASONRY	PER SF	$15-$25	*
EXTERIOR PAINTING			
PAINT EXTERIOR	PER FLOOR SF	$1.50-$3.00	*
PAINT EXTERIOR TRIM	PER FLOOR SF	$.50-$1.00	*
DECKS/PORCHES			
BUILD DECK	PER SF	$18-$30	*
CONCRETE			
LARGE CONCRETE JOBS	PER SF	$5-$10	*
SMALL CONCRETE JOBS	PER SF	$5-$10	*
GARAGE			
REPLACE GARAGE DOOR	PER DOOR	$500-$1,200	*
REPLACE DOOR OPENER	PER OPENER	$200-$400	*
LANDSCAPING			
LAWN MAINTENANCE	PER 1/4 ACRE	$30-$60	*
TRIM BUSHES	PER YARD	$30-$60	*
TRIM TREE	PER TREE	$100-$250	*
REMOVE TREE	PER TREE	$100-$1,500	*

TASK	UNIT	LABOR	MATERIALS
INSTALL SOD	PER SF	$1-$2	*
BUILD RETAINING WALL			
CONCRETE BLOCK WALL	PER SF	$30-$50	*
WOOD WALL	PER SF	$20-$40	*
STONE WALL	PER SF	$30-$50	*
POURED CONCRETE WALL	PER SF	$30-$50	*
HEAVY EQUIPMENT WORK	PER DAY	$1,000-$2,000	*
SEPTIC SYSTEM			
INSPECT/CLEAN SEPTIC TANK	PER TANK	$300-$500	*
MAJOR SEPTIC REPAIRS	PER REPAIR	$1,000-$10,000+	*
FOUNDATION			
ENGINEER CONSULTATION	PER HOUR	$75-$150	*
FIX FOUNDATION WALL	PER LF	$100-$300	*
OTHER FOUNDATION REPAIR	PER REPAIR	$500-$10,000+	*
DEMO			
ROLL-OFF DUMPSTER	DUMPSTER	$300-$600	*
DEMO LABOR			
SMALL JOBS	PER HOUR	$10-$15	*
FULL DEMO	PER SF	$.50-$1.00	*

TASK	UNIT	LABOR	MATERIALS
PORTA POTTY	PER MONTH	$100-$200	*
PLUMBING			
SERVICE CALL	PER HOUR	$60-$100	*
REPLACE MAIN LINE	PER HOUSE	$1,500-$3,000	*
REPLACE PRV	PER HOUSE	$150-$300	*
REPLACE WATER HEATER	PER HOUSE	$150-$250	$400-$800
REPLACE ALL SUPPLY LINES	PER FIXTURE	$250-$350	*
INSTALL/REPLACE TUB	PER TUB	$250-$500	$300-$600
BUILD TILE SHOWER	PER SF	$20-$30	$3-$10
INSTALL/REPLACE SINK			
KITCHEN SINK	PER SINK	$50-$100	$40-$150
BATHROOM SINK	PER SINK	$40-$80	$30-$60
INSTALL/REPLACE FAUCET	PER FAUCET		
KITCHEN FAUCET	PER SINK	$40-$80	$80-$200
BATHROOM FAUCET	PER SINK	$40-$80	$20-$60
INSTALL TUB/SHOWER HARDWARE			
TRIM KIT ONLY	PER TUB	$40-$80	$50-$100
TRIM KIT + MIXER	PER TUB	$80-$150	$80-$200
INSTALL/REPLACE TOILET	PER TOILET	$60-$100	$100-$200

TASK	UNIT	LABOR	MATERIALS
REPLACE WASHER BOX	PER BOX	$150-$250	*
INSTALL DISHWASHER	PER HOUSE	$80-$150	SEE APPLIANCES
FIX LEAK			
ABOVE SLAB	PER LINE	$80-$250	*
BELOW SLAB	PER LINE	$200-$1,000+	*
UNCLOG DRAIN	PER DRAIN	$80-$150	*
ELECTRICAL			
SERVICE CALL	PER HOUR	$60-$100	*
UPGRADE SERVICE	PER HOUSE	$1,200-$2,500	*
REPLACE CIRCUIT PANEL	PER PANEL	$800-$1,500	*
REWIRE HOUSE	PER FIXTURE	$50-$100	*
ADD NEW CIRCUIT	PER CIRCUIT	$125-$250	*
ADD NEW OUTLET/BOX	PER OUTLET	$60-$100	*
UPGRADE OUTLET TO GFCI	PER OUTLET	$30-$50	*
ADD NEW SWITCH	PER SWITCH	$100-$150	*
INSTALL CAN LIGHT	PER CAN	$60-$100	*
INSTALL LIGHT	PER LIGHT	$30-$60	$10 AND UP
INSTALL FAN	PER FAN	$40-$70	$20 AND UP
REPLACE OUTLET/SWITCH	PER OUTLET	$5-$10	*

TASK	UNIT	LABOR	MATERIALS
HVAC			
SERVICE CALL	PER HOUR	$60-$100	*
HVAC MAINTENANCE	PER SYSTEM	$150-$200	*
INSTALL FORCED-AIR SYSTEM	PER SYSTEM	$5,000-$8,000	*
REPLACE FURNACE	PER UNIT	$1,000-$2,000	*
REPLACE COMPRESSOR AND COIL			
COMPRESSOR ONLY	PER UNIT	$1,200-$2,000	*
COMPRESSOR AND COIL	PER UNIT	$1,800-$3,000	*
REPLACE HEAT PUMP	PER UNIT	$2,000-$3,500	*
FRAMING			
FRAME WALLS	PER LF	$6-$12	$5-$8
FRAME HOUSE	PER FLOOR SF	$4-$12	$6-$12
INSULATION			
INSTALL INSULATION			
LOOSE-FILL INSULATION	PER SF	$1-$2	*
BATT/BLANKET INSULATION	PER LF	$1-$2	*
RIGID BOARD INSULATION	PER SF	$1-$2	*
SPRAY FOAM INSULATION	PER SF	$2-$5	*

TASK	UNIT	LABOR	MATERIALS
SHEETROCK			
PREP SHEETROCK FOR PAINT	PER HOUSE	$0-$500	*
PATCH SHEETROCK	PER HOUSE	$0-$500	*
INSTALL NEW SHEETROCK			
WALL BOARD	PER SF	$1.00-$1.50	*
NON-WALL BOARD	PER SF	$1.20-$1.70	*
APPLY TEXTURE	PER SF	$.05-$.25	*
CARPENTRY			
BASIC CARPENTRY	PER HOUR	$25-$35	
INSTALL DOOR			
EXTERIOR DOOR	PER DOOR	$100-$175	$150-$300
INTERIOR DOOR	PER DOOR	$30-$50	$40-$90
FRENCH DOOR	PER DOOR	$150-$200	$300-$600
SLIDING GLASS DOOR	PER DOOR	$150-$250	$300-$600
REPLACE WINDOW	PER WINDOW	$75-$110	$100-$200
FINISH TRIM	PER FLOOR SF	$1.00-$1.50	SEE BELOW
	PER LF	SEE ABOVE	$.75-$1.50
INTERIOR PAINTING			
PAINT INTERIOR			
REPAINT	PER FLOOR SF	$1.50-$2.25	*

TASK	UNIT	LABOR	MATERIALS
PAINT NEW SHEETROCK	PER FLOOR SF	$1.25-$2.70	*
CABINETS/COUNTERTOPS			
INSTALL KITCHEN CABINETS	PER LF	$40-$60	$100-$250
INSTALL BATHROOM VANITIES	PER VANITY	$75-$100	$100-$400
INSTALL COUNTERTOPS			
LAMINATE COUNTERTOPS	PER LF	$18-$22	*
GRANITE COUNTERTOPS	PER SF	$35-$50	*
FLOORING			
REPLACE SUBFLOOR	PER SF	$.60-$.85	$.75-$1.00
INSTALL VINYL/LINOLEUM			
ROLLED VINYL	PER SY	$4-$6	$8-$12
VINYL SQUARES	PER SF	$1.00-$1.50	$1-$2
INSTALL CARPET/PAD	PER SY	$4-$7	SEE BELOW
CARPET MATERIAL	PER SY	SEE ABOVE	$10-$18
PAD MATERIAL	PER SY	SEE ABOVE	$2-$3
CLEAN CARPET	PER ROOM	$50-$80	
INSTALL LAMINATE WOOD	PER SF	$1.50-$3.50	$.50-$3.50
INSTALL ENGINEERED WOOD	PER SF	$1.50-$3.50	$1-$5
INSTALL SOLID WOOD (PRE-FINISH)	PER SF	$1.50-$3.50	$2-$5

TASK	UNIT	LABOR	MATERIALS
INSTALL SOLID WOOD (SITE-FINISH)	PER SF	$3-$4	$1.50-$4.50
REFINISH HARDWOOD	PER SF	$1.50-$2.00	*
INSTALL TILE	PER SF	$3-$6	$1-$10
PERMITS			
PERMIT DRAWINGS	PER HOUR	$40-$70	*
PERMITS	PER HOUSE	$35-$2,000	*
INSPECTIONS	PER INSPECTION	$50-$100	*
GENERAL CONTRACTOR FEES	PER PROJECT	7%-15%	*
MOLD			
AIR QUALITY TEST (AQT)	PER TEST	$100-$200	*
MOLD REMEDIATION	PER HOUSE	$500-$10,000+	*
TERMITES			
TERMITE INSPECTION	PER INSPECTION	FREE	*
TERMITE TREATMENT			
BAITING TREATMENT	PER LF	$4-$6	*
CHEMICAL TREATMENT	PER LF	$4-$6	*
FUMIGATION	PER FLOOR SF	$1-$2	*
TERMITE LETTER	PER LETTER	$35-$100	*

TASK	UNIT	LABOR	MATERIALS
MISCELLANEOUS			
MISCELLANEOUS TASKS	PER HOUSE	$250-$1,000	$250-$1,000
APPLIANCES			
REFRIGERATOR	PER APPLIANCE	*	$500-$900
RANGE	PER APPLIANCE	*	$500-$700
DISHWASHER	PER APPLIANCE	SEE PLUMBING	$300-$500
MICROWAVE	PER APPLIANCE	$40-$60	$150-$250
WASHER/DRYER SET	PER SET	*	$800-$1,000
HOUSE CLEANING	PER HOUSE	$100-$250	*

ACKNOWLEDGEMENTS

A book like this is never written in a vacuum. It requires the support, dedication, and input of dozens of people, and I'd like to take a moment to thank those who have helped to make this book possible.

First and foremost, a never-ending thank you to my amazingly supportive wife, Carol—you make everything I do easier and more fun, and without you, we never would have started on the journey that has led me to this book.

Next, I have to thank all of the generous investors around the country who were kind enough to provide me (sometimes proprietary) information from the business that led to the price ranges in this book. Dozens of you spent copious amounts of time filling out questionnaires and answering my follow-up questions, leading to all the data encapsulated in this book.

Specifically, thank you to:

Nathan Rosenberg	ScottBuilt
Brian Silverman	Scott Silver Homes
Todd Whiddon	VanderBuilt Homes
Sean Sweeney	Hayes Harlow
Matt Rodak	Fund That Flip
Tarl Yarber	Fixated Real Estate
Matt & Liz Faircloth	DeRosa Group

Curt Davis	Buy Memphis Now
Bryan Blankenship	Ohio Cash Buyers, LLC
Justin Silverio	JS2 Homes LLC
Alexander Felice	BrokeIsAChoice.com
D.J. Cummins	D & E Cummins, LLC
Charlie Kao	MCK Management
Steven Dannenmann	SD Investment Properties, LLC
Mark Graffagnino	Ashford Contractors
Matt Maurice	REIS Property Management
Simeon Zabchev	IC Invest, LLC
Vadim Shapiro	Centerstone Properties
Tim & Kareen Tooker	Homes By Tooker
Robert Foor	Homes By Tooker
Matt Rembish	Persistence Properties
Dave Rembish	Persistence Properties
Christine Rembish	Persistence Properties
Josh & Lizzie Parra	Parra Design & Build
Scott Hollister	David Wesley Real Estate, LLC
Aaron Foster	Hometown Heroes REI
Garrett Hogan	OnPoint Capital
George Bittar	GeorgeBittar.com
Christina Ramirez	R2InvestmentGroup, LLC
Ceasar Rosas	C2C Homes LLC
Dr. Kristen Ray	Vytal Investments, LLC
Rob & Alison Loiselle	FiveTen Properties LLC
Gene Murashko	Murashko Family Homes LLC
Bobby Ureno Jr.	Omnicon Investments LLC
Matt Hedstrom	Sell Fast with Us
Steve Sparks	Rebound Properties, LLC
Gabe DaSilva	DaSilva Homes
Jeremiah Dalton	Suffolk County House Buyers
Nadiya Lonkevych	

A special thank you as well to the more than a dozen investors who provided their support but preferred to remain anonymous and not be mentioned by name in these acknowledgements.

Finally, a special thanks to Josh Dorkin, Scott Trench, Katie Askew, Brandon Turner, and everyone at BiggerPockets and BiggerPockets Publishing. A lot of time, effort, and patience went into building a great partnership that has led to this book, and each of you was instrumental in fostering that partnership. I look forward to working with each of you many times over.

Finally, thank you to the editors, designers, and proofreaders who made this book worth reading: Thomas Hauck (Line Editing/Proofreading), Katie Golownia (Proofreading), Wendy Dunning (Layout), Jarrod Jemison (Cover Design), and Kaylee Pratt, who worked hard on the marketing to get this book into your hands.

ABOUT THE AUTHOR

J Scott (he goes by "J") is a full-time real estate investor and rehabber living in the suburbs of Washington, D.C. He is originally from the East Coast, and until spring of 2008, he resided in Silicon Valley, California, where he spent many years in management at several Fortune 500 companies.

In 2008, J and his wife decided to leave the 80-hour workweeks and the constant business travel behind. They quit their corporate jobs, moved back East, started a family, and decided to try something new. That something new ended up being real estate, and a decade later, they've built a successful business buying, rehabbing, and reselling single-family homes.

Since 2008, J and his wife have rehabbed over 150 of their own houses for millions in profits and have partnered with, mentored, and assisted other investors in rehabbing hundreds more properties. These days, the team has branched out, now flipping houses in different parts of the country and focusing on larger new construction projects.

J has detailed his real estate adventure on his blog: www.123flip.com, where he discusses all his team's triumphs, failures, and results—including all the nitty-gritty financial details of the business.

J can be reached at questions@123flip.com.

More from
BiggerPockets Publishing

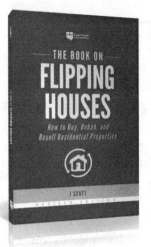

The Book on Flipping Houses

Written by active real estate investor and fix-and-flipper J Scott, this book contains more than 300 pages of detailed step-by-step training perfect for both the complete newbie and the seasoned pro looking to build a killer house-flipping business. Whatever your skill level, this book will teach you everything you need to know to build a profitable business to start living the life of your dreams.

Real Estate Note Investing

Are you a wholesaler, a rehabber, a landlord, or even a turnkey investor? *Real Estate Note Investing* will help you turn your focus to the "other side" of real estate investing, allowing you to make money without tenants, toilets, and termites! Investing in notes is the easiest strategy to make passive income. Learn the ins-and-outs of notes as investor Dave Van Horn shows you how to get started—and find huge success—in the powerful world of real estate notes!

If you enjoyed this book, we hope you'll take a moment to check out some of the other great material BiggerPockets offers. BiggerPockets is the real estate investing social network, marketplace, and information hub, designed to help make you a smarter real estate investor through podcasts, books, blog posts, videos, forums, and more. Sign up today—it's free! **Visit www.BiggerPockets.com.**

The Book on Rental Property Investing

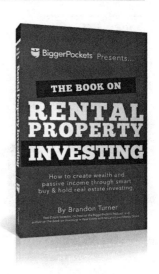

The Book on Rental Property Investing, written by Brandon Turner, a real estate investor and cohost of the *BiggerPockets Podcast*, contains nearly 400 pages of in-depth advice and strategies for building wealth through rental properties. You'll learn how to build an achievable plan, find incredible deals, pay for your rentals, and much more! If you've ever thought of using rental properties to build wealth or obtain financial freedom, this book is for you.

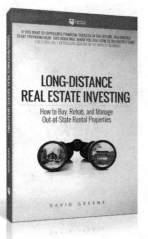

Long-Distance Real Estate Investing

Don't let your location dictate your financial freedom: Live where you want, and invest anywhere it makes sense! The rules, technology, and markets have changed: No longer are you forced to invest only in your backyard. In *Long-Distance Real Estate Investing*, learn an in-depth strategy to build profitable rental portfolios through buying, managing, and flipping out-of-state properties from real estate investor and agent David Greene.

More from
BiggerPockets Publishing

The Book on Investing in Real Estate with No (and Low) Money Down

Lack of money holding you back from real estate success? It doesn't have to! In this groundbreaking book from Brandon Turner, author of *The Book on Rental Property Investing*, you'll discover numerous strategies investors can use to buy real estate using other people's money. You'll learn the top strategies that savvy investors are using to buy, rent, flip, or wholesale properties at scale!

Retire Early with Real Estate

Are you stuck in the rut of a 9-to-5 job? Would you like to do more with your life than just work to pay the bills? *Retire Early with Real Estate* provides practical, proven methods to quickly and safely build wealth using the time-tested vehicle of real estate rentals. Experienced real estate investor and early retiree, Chad Carson, shares his tried-and-true investment strategies to create enough passive income to retire at 37 years old.

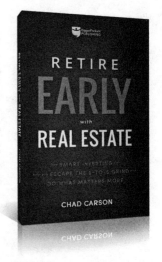

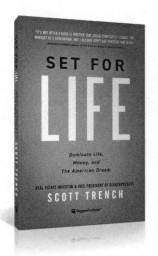

Set for Life: Dominate Life, Money, and the American Dream

Looking for a plan to achieve financial freedom in just five to ten years? *Set for Life* is a detailed fiscal plan targeted at the median-income earner starting with few or no assets. It will walk you through three stages of finance, guiding you to your first $25,000 in tangible net worth, then to your first $100,000, and then to financial freedom. *Set for Life* will teach you how to build a lifestyle, career, and investment portfolio capable of supporting financial freedom to let you live the life of your dreams.

Raising Private Capital

Are you ready to help other investors build their wealth while you build your real estate empire? The road map outlined in *Raising Private Capital* helps investors looking to inject more private capital into their business—the most effective strategy for growth! Author and investor Matt Faircloth helps you learn how to develop long-term wealth from his valuable lessons and experiences in real estate: Get the truth behind the wins and losses from someone who has experienced it all.

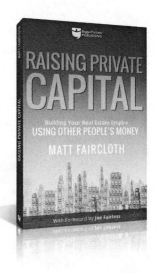

CONNECT WITH BIGGERPOCKETS
and Become Successful in Your Real Estate Business Today!

Facebook
/BiggerPockets

Instagram
@BiggerPockets

Twitter
@BiggerPockets

LinkedIn
/company/Bigger
Pockets

Website
BiggerPockets.com